engage

It's the fourth issue of **engage**, and it's stuffed with even more Bible-y goodness and thought-provoking articles than usual. Check out what's in store for you inside. In this issue...

DAILY READINGS Each day's page throws you into the Bible, to get you handling, questioning and exploring God's message to you — encouraging you to act on it and talk to God more in prayer.

THIS ISSUE: God's spectacular rescue in **Exodus**; the power of the gospel in **2 Timothy**; God's greatness in **Psalms**; Jesus' incredible final words in **John's Gospel**; is life really meaningless? **Ecclesiastes** gives us the answers.

ESSENTIAL Articles on the basics we really need to know about God, the Bible and Christianity. This time we focus on the **Holy Spirit.**

TAKE IT FURTHER If you're left wanting more at the end of an **engage** page, turn to the **Take it further** section to dig deeper.

REAL LIVES Amazing true stories, revealing God at work in people's lives. This time — **the teenager who was killed for his faith.**

STUFF Articles on stuff relevant to young Christians. This time: what's the Bible say about **self-esteem?**

TOOLBOX is full of tools to help you wrestle with the Bible and understand it for yourself. This issue we look at **the missing link.**

TRICKY tackles those mind-bendingly tricky questions that confuse us all, as well as questions that our friends bombard us with. This issue: **Did the resurrection really happen?**

All of us who work on **engage** are passionate to see God's Word at work in people's lives. Do you want God's Word to have an impact on your life? Then open your Bible, and start on the first **engage** study right now...

1 Set a time you can read the Bible every day

2 Find a place where you can be quiet and think

3 Grab your Bible, pen and a notebook

4 Ask God to help you understand what you read

5 Read the day's verses with **engage**, taking time to think about it

6 Pray about what you've read

BIBLE STUFF We use the NIV Bible version, so you might find it's the best one to use with **engage**. If the notes say **'Read Exodus 1 v 15–22'**, look up Exodus in the contents page at the front of your Bible. It'll tell you which page Exodus starts on. Find chapter 1 of Exodus, and then verse 15 of chapter 1 (the verse numbers are the tiny ones). Then start reading!

In this issue...

DAILY READINGS

Exodus: God to the rescue

2 Timothy: Letter from death row

John: Famous last words

Ecclesiastes: Everything's meaningless!

Psalms: Bombarded by brilliance

ARTICLES

STUFF
Self-esteem **20**

REAL LIVES
Killed for Christ **36**

ESSENTIAL
That's the Spirit **44**

TOOLBOX
The missing link **60**

TRICKY
Did the resurrection happen? **90**

ENGAGE EGGHEADS

Scribblers: Martin Cole   Cassie Martin   Adrian Taylor–Weekes
          Tim Thornborough   Helen Thorne
Excited editor: Martin Cole
Dazzling design: Steve Devane
Expert proof-reading: Anne Woodcock

Exodus

Exit strategy

Welcome to the second book of
the Bible. Exodus means 'exit'
or 'departure'. It's all about God
getting His people out of Egypt.
In spectacular style.

WAY OUT?

In Engage 3 we saw God put His man
Joseph in Egypt so that God's people
would be able to get food and survive
years of crippling drought. But how
would they get out of Egypt — where
they were treated like dirt by the
locals — and get to the land God had
promised them?

EXIT SIGNS

Step forward Moses, the reluctant
hero of Exodus, who God would
use in amazing ways to show the
Israelites the way to the exit.

HISTORY LESSON

So it's all just ancient history, right?
Wrong — Christians today have been
rescued by God too, through Jesus'
death and resurrection. So we'll see
how Exodus sets the scene for what
Jesus did.

**This poses the big question:
if you've been rescued by God,
are you living His way right now?**

1

Exterminate!

Sometimes things just seem to go from bad to worse. The Israelites were stuck in Egypt, ruled over cruelly by the Egyptians. But things would get much worse before they got better.

👁 Read Exodus 1 v 1–14

ENGAGE YOUR BRAIN
▶ *What was going well for the Israelites? (v7)*
▶ *What did the Egyptians fear?(v10)*
▶ *How did they react? (v14)*

God had chosen a bunch of people — the Israelites — to be His special people. He'd promised Abraham that He'd look after them, give them loads of kids, a homeland in Israel and that through these people the whole world would be blessed (Genesis 12 v 1–3).

And to help them survive a famine, God engineered it so that they ended up in Egypt, where He'd placed His man Joseph to organise food supplies. Clever!

The Israelites were growing rapidly, just as God had promised. This panicked the Egyptians, who tried to grind them down with forced labour. But it didn't seem to work — they just kept growing (v12). So Pharaoh took desperate measures.

👁 Read verses 15–22
▶ *What did Pharaoh order? (v16)*
▶ *But what happened?*
▶ *What's Exodus already teaching us about God? (v20–21)*

God had a plan for His people and, despite the Egyptians extreme cruelty, God's plans would not be stopped. We can already see a glimpse of His rescue, His love and His compassion for His people.

PRAY ABOUT IT
Ask God to show you His awe-inspiring love, compassion and rescue as you read Exodus.

THE BOTTOM LINE
God looks out for His people.

→ TAKE IT FURTHER
Want a little more? Then go to **Take it further** on page 109.

2

God's people, the Israelites, are living in harsh conditions in Egypt. Pharaoh is worried about them getting out of control so he's ordered every Israelite baby to be thrown into the River Nile as soon as it's born.

👁 Read Exodus 2 v 1–4

ENGAGE YOUR BRAIN

▶ *What desperate measures did the baby's mother take?*

This couple were Levites, one of the 12 Israelite tribes. When the woman gave birth to a boy they must have been devastated, knowing he'd have to die. She tried to keep him hidden, but in the end sent him to float down the river in a watertight basket.

👁 Read verses 5–10

▶ *Who rescued the tot?*

▶ *Flick back to Exodus 1 v 22. What might she have done with him?*

▶ *What else worked out brilliantly? (v7–9)*

Unbelievably, baby Moses was protected by an Egyptian! Pharaoh's daughter took pity on the little mite, even though he was a Hebrew (Israelite). God had big plans for

Moses: He kept Moses alive, got his own mother to look after him, and he was brought up as an Egyptian. This boy was special, and God would use him in surprising ways.

Throughout the Bible we read about God's enemies attacking and trying to destroy God's people. But God is in control, and He will never be wiped out. In fact, they will survive to live eternally with God.

PRAY ABOUT IT
Thank God that He's with His people even through the toughest of times. Thank Him that no one can destroy His people.

THE BOTTOM LINE
God's people will not be destroyed.

➡ TAKE IT FURTHER
Appetite for destruction? Page 109.

3 | On the run

Imagine being born in one country but growing up in a totally different one. Where would your loyalties lie? Moses had Hebrew parents but was brought up as an Egyptian. Let's see where his heart was...

👁 Read Exodus 2 v 11–15

ENGAGE YOUR BRAIN

▶ Who did Moses side with?

▶ What do you think about his actions and motives? (v12)

▶ What were the consequences? (v14–15)

Despite being brought up in Pharaoh's family, Moses knew who his people were (v11). When he saw how cruelly the Egyptians treated Hebrews, he snapped. His murderous anger caused him to have to flee Egypt in a hurry. How could God possibly use this runaway killer?

👁 Read verses 16–22

▶ How did things work out for Moses?

Moses ran for his life into the desert. But God was looking after him and led him to a friendly family, and even a wife and son.

THINK IT THROUGH

▶ Do you believe God can use **you**?

▶ Do you think you're too sinful to serve God?

God often uses weak, sinful people in His plans. Moses had killed a man, yet God kept him safe and would still use him to rescue His people.

Don't limit God. He can do anything, including using seemingly useless people like us. He can use us to spread the gospel and to serve other Christians. The question is, are you ready to let Him use you?

PRAY ABOUT IT

If you actually mean it, ask God to use you in His big plans. But be warned, He will!

THE BOTTOM LINE

God uses the least likely people.

➔ TAKE IT FURTHER

Back to school on page 109.

Cry for help

Family illness. Depression. Natural disasters. Suffering. It's often in the darkest times that people turn to God for help.

👁 Read Exodus 2 v 23–25

ENGAGE YOUR BRAIN

▶ What are we told about the Israelites?

▶ What do we learn about God?

▶ What did God remember?

The Israelites in Egypt were being treated brutally by the Egyptians — living in slavery, forced to do back-breaking work, and many of their children were drowned at birth. In this moment of great suffering, they cried out to God for help.

👁 Read Genesis 17 v 6–8

▶ What did God promise Abraham?

v6:

v7:

v8:

When the Israelites groaned to God, He remembered His covenant agreement with Abraham. God had promised to make Abraham's family into a great nation, giving them the land of Canaan. He would be their God.

The Israelites were God's people — He loved them and would keep His promises as always. He would rescue them from slavery.

PRAY ABOUT IT

God promises to be with all of His people. He hears our prayers too and is concerned for us. Use Exodus 2 v 24–25 to thank God for what He's like.

THE BOTTOM LINE

God hears His people's cries.

→ TAKE IT FURTHER

Prayer pointers on page 109.

7

5 Warning: bush fire

The Israelites cried out to God to free them from slavery. By now, Moses was pushing 80 years old, minding his own business, looking after sheep in Midian. He wouldn't have expected to get the big call-up from God.

👁 Read Exodus 3 v 1–6

ENGAGE YOUR BRAIN

▶ *What was Moses required to do in God's presence? (v5)*

▶ *How did God introduce Himself? (v6)*

▶ *How did Moses react to that?*

God grabbed Moses' attention in a bizarre way — a bush on fire that didn't burn up. It worked. God let Moses know exactly who was speaking to Him: the God of his ancestors.

No wonder Moses was terrified. He took off his sandals to show respect for God in His presence. And he hid his face, completely humbled by the perfect, holy God of all history.

👁 Read verses 7–10

▶ *How would v7 have encouraged Moses?*

▶ *But what was the shock news for Moses? (v10)*

The Lord promised a great future for His people — freed from slavery and taken into a land overflowing with the good life (v8). Moses must have been thrilled. Until God gave him the job of rescuer. Panic attack time. We'll look at Moses' reaction tomorrow.

TALK IT THROUGH

▶ *Do you show God enough respect?*

▶ *What do you need to change about the way you talk to God or talk about God?*

PRAY ABOUT IT

If you're a Christian, God has called you too — to spread the word about Jesus and to serve Him throughout your life. Ask God to help you do what He wants you to do.

→ TAKE IT FURTHER

Into the fire — page 109.

6

I AM WHO AM

Things are starting to kick off. The Israelites cried out to God to rescue them. God appeared to Moses in a burning bush, telling him to bring God's people out of Egypt. But Moses wasn't too excited about the job...

👁 Read Exodus 3 v 11–12

ENGAGE YOUR BRAIN

▶ What was Moses' first excuse?

▶ What did God say to reassure him?

Moses didn't think he was the right man for the job. But God said: *'I'll be with you, so trust me.'* Only once the Israelites were out of Egypt would Moses fully realise it was the work of God (v12).

👁 Read verses 13–15

▶ What was Moses' second excuse?

▶ What fantastic truth was Moses to tell the people? (v14–15)

The awesome name for God: **I AM**. The one who is, forever. The God of His people — past, present and future (v15). He was Abraham, Isaac and Jacob's God, and He would always be the God of the Israelites. Astonishing stuff.

The God of the Israelites is our God too. He has always existed. He is perfect and will never change. And He will rule His people for ever.

PRAY ABOUT IT

Take time out to praise God for what His name means.

THE BOTTOM LINE

God is, was and always will be. He's the God of the past, present and future, who will always be with His people.

→ TAKE IT FURTHER

More about **I AM** on page 110.

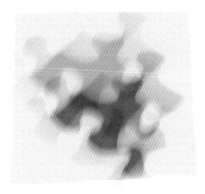

7 Back to the future

Calendars are usually filled with scribbles detailing all your future plans. Today in Exodus we get to see what God has planned for the Israelites. Not only the events, but the results too!

● Read Exodus 3 v 16–22

ENGAGE YOUR BRAIN

▶ How would all this info encourage Moses?

▶ Describe the series of events:

v16–18:

v18–19:

v20:

v21–22:

What an amazing response to the Israelites' cries for help. God promised to rescue them in a spectacular way. God even told Moses exactly how He would do it, so they could look back and see how God had kept His promises. To the letter.

Yesterday we read how God is the great I AM: He has always existed, He never changes and He'll rule for ever. God knows everything that has happened and everything that will happen. So He could tell Moses what would happen to the Israelites.

GET ON WITH IT

Ever tempted by horoscopes or fortune-telling to find out about the future? Throw them out of your life — they're pointless. God knows all about you. He knows what plans He has for you in the future. We don't need horoscopes — we have a perfect God in control of our future.

PRAY ABOUT IT

Thank God that your future is safe in His hands. Ask Him to use you to serve Him loads in the future.

THE BOTTOM LINE

God knows and controls the future.

➔ TAKE IT FURTHER

Step into the future on page 110.

8

Excuse me

Are you a willing volunteer who's happy to get stuck into anything, or do you prefer to hide in the background? God had promised to use Moses to free the Israelites from slavery, but Moses was full of excuses.

Read Exodus 4 v 1–9

ENGAGE YOUR BRAIN

D *What was Moses' excuse?*

D *What three signs would God give him as proof?*

Moses was trying to wriggle out of his responsibilities. But God was patient with Moses and gave him proof to show the leaders that he really had met God. But Moses was desperate to get out of it...

Read verses 10–17

D *What were Moses' two last desperate excuses? (v10, 13)*

D *How did God respond to Moses' lack of trust? (v14–16)*

Moses let his doubts in his own abilities lead to him not trusting God. The Lord can do anything (v11). Of course he could use cowardly Moses. God was angry with Moses' lack of trust, yet still showed

incredible patience and reassured Moses by getting his bro Aaron to help him.

GET ON WITH IT

D *What responsibilities are you avoiding at the mo?*

D *What excuses are you using for not fully serving God?*

D *Do you let self-doubt stop you obeying God?*

PRAY ABOUT IT

Bring these things before God right now. Ask Him to help you trust Him to give you the strength and abilities to serve Him.

THE BOTTOM LINE

Stop making excuses with God.

→ TAKE IT FURTHER

No excuses... go to page 110.

9

The wanderer returns

Years ago, Moses had fled from Egypt after killing an Egyptian. Finally, he was about to return — this time to rescue God's people from slavery. But would the Israelites trust God and follow Moses?

👁 Read Exodus 4 v 18–23

ENGAGE YOUR BRAIN

▶ What was the good news for Moses? (v19)

▶ What was the bad news? (v21)

▶ What did God call the Israelites? (v22)

God encouraged Moses that it was safe for him to go back to Egypt, so Moses grabbed his family and left. The bad news was that despite Moses performing miracles in front of Pharaoh, he would still refuse to let God's people go. But the Israelites were God's chosen people and God would care for them (v22) and punish Pharaoh for his unbelief (v23).

👁 Read verses 24–26

What a bizarre story. It seems that Moses hadn't circumcised his son (as God had commanded His people to do in Genesis 17 v 9–14) and faced God's punishment. Zipporah saved the day by doing the deed herself and associating Moses with it (v25).

👁 Read verses 27–31

▶ How did the Israelite elders respond to Moses and Aaron?

▶ Had Moses been right to worry and try to get out of it?

Aaron was now onboard to help Moses. And so were the Israelite leaders. When they realised that God had heard their prayers, they bowed down in worship

PRAY ABOUT IT

▶ Have you seen God answer your prayers?

▶ Do you know that He loves you?

▶ So what will you say to Him right now?

➔ TAKE IT FURTHER

Hard hearts on page 110.

10

I‾ ‾ ‾ ‾ ‾ ‾ ‾ ‾ ‾ ‾ ‾ ‾ ‾ ‾ ‾ ‾ I
| The final straw |
I_ _ _ _ _ _ _ _ _ _ _ _ _ _ _I

Moses has returned to Egypt to free God's people from slavery. The Israelite leaders are behind him. So far. But now Moses is going to face up to hard-hearted Pharaoh (Amunhotep II) for the first time.

👁 **Read Exodus 5 v 1–9**

ENGAGE YOUR BRAIN

▶ What did God (through Moses) demand from Pharaoh? (v1)

▶ What was Pharaoh's response? (v2, v4–5)

▶ How was he even more 'unfair-oh'? (v6–9)

The Israelites must have got their hopes up. They'd seen Moses and Aaron perform miracles in front of their eyes. Now these two were going to meet Pharaoh and lead God's people out of Egypt! But it wouldn't be that easy. In fact, Pharaoh was going to make it as difficult as he could, making their hard work impossible to do. Make bricks without straw? No chance!

👁 **Read verses 10–21**

▶ What effect did Pharaoh's cruel work rules have?

▶ What was the Israelites' attitude towards Moses and Aaron now?

Pharaoh's clever ruse to turn God's people against Moses and Aaron had the desired effect. The Israelite leaders were dejected and they blamed M & A. Their trust in God to free them disappeared. Tomorrow we'll see God's response.

God didn't promise that Moses' task would be easy. In fact, it now seemed impossible, yet God's promise to rescue the Israelites stood. But it wasn't down to Moses. Despite this impossible situation, God would keep His promises and everyone would see His power.

PRAY ABOUT IT

Ask God to help you trust Him even when things are going badly. And pray for Christian leaders who face opposition despite serving God.

➡ TAKE IT FURTHER

A little bit more on page 110.

11 | Powerful promises

Have you ever got angry with God? Pointed the finger of blame at Him? What causes you to doubt God and His promises? Moses felt useless and rejected and let down by God.

👁 Read Exodus 5 v 22–23

ENGAGE YOUR BRAIN

- ▶ *How would you describe Moses' attitude to God?*
- ▶ *What had he forgotten about God?*

👁 Read Exodus 6 v 1–5

- ▶ *How did God reassure Moses? (v1)*
- ▶ *What reminders did God give to encourage him? (v2–5)*

Incredibly encouraging words from God. The Lord *would* rescue His people (v1). Maybe not immediately, but He would do it. God would keep the promises He made to Moses' ancestors, giving the Israelites a land of their own (v4). Amazingly, God had revealed more of His character to Moses than He had to Abraham and the rest (v3).

👁 Read verses 6–12

- ▶ *What dramatic promises did God make? (v6–8)*

- ▶ *How would these things happen?*
- ▶ *How did the people respond?*

God's promises to His people were phenomenal. But they were so caught up in their current sadness they refused to believe God. And this got Moses down and he doubted God again. Oh dear.

SHARE IT

- ▶ *Who do you know who has stopped trusting God?*
- ▶ *What examples of God's faithfulness in the past can you point them to?*

PRAY ABOUT IT

Thank God that He keeps His promises. Thank Him for things He's done in the past that show He's totally faithful.

THE BOTTOM LINE

Don't doubt God. He always delivers.

➔ TAKE IT FURTHER

Trust me, you should go to page 110.

12

Feeling listless?

How are you with lists? Or family trees? Do they get you strangely excited or does your brain collapse through boredom? Try to work out if this list of names in Exodus has any relevance at all.

👁 Read Exodus 6 v 13–27

ENGAGE YOUR BRAIN

▶ *What did this list tell people about Aaron and Moses? (v26–7)*

This family roll call told people exactly who A & M were. They were just ordinary Israelites who God would use to do sensational things. And it's a nice reminder that God got these guys in position long before the Exodus. It was all part of God's perfect plans.

👁 Read Exodus 6 v 28 – 7 v 7

▶ *What was Moses to do? (v1–2)*

▶ *What would Pharaoh do? (v4)*

▶ *What would God do? (v5)*

In Old Testament times, God spoke to His people through prophets. In the same way, Moses would give God's message to Pharaoh via the lips of Aaron, acting as a prophet.

God commanded Moses and Aaron to deliver His message to Pharaoh even though they knew Pharaoh wouldn't listen to them. Sometimes telling people about Jesus can be tough like that. They refuse to listen to us. But that's no reason to give up. They still need to hear the message of Jesus and God wants us to keep plugging away.

SHARE IT

▶ *Who do you find it hard to share the gospel with?*

▶ *Who will you resolve to talk to about Jesus again?*

PRAY ABOUT IT

Talk to God about how tough it is, and ask Him to help you not give up.

THE BOTTOM LINE

Keep delivering God's message.

➔ TAKE IT FURTHER

Spread the word on page 111.

15

13 | Flood of blood

Ever had a conversation (or maybe a full-blooded argument) where you just can't seem to get your point across? The other person refuses to agree with a word you say and you end up so frustrated. Aaaaarrrrrrghhh!

👁 **Read Exodus 7 v 8–13**

ENGAGE YOUR BRAIN

▶ What did Aaron do as proof he was sent by God?

▶ Were Pharaoh's wise guys more powerful? (v12)

Aaron's staff transformed into a snake — it was a sign to Pharaoh that A & M had been sent by God. It was also a sign of God's great power.

For a moment, it looked as if the magicians were just as powerful — until Aaron's snake munched theirs! Despite this, Pharaoh wouldn't listen to them, just as God had said he wouldn't.

👁 **Read verses 14–25**

▶ What should this plague have taught Pharaoh? (v16–17)

▶ What was Pharaoh's reaction? (v22–23)

Try to imagine the whole revolting scene. The Egyptians worshipped the River Nile as a god. But God's men, Moses and Aaron, turned it to blood. In fact, all the water (even in buckets and jars) became bloody and undrinkable. It was a sign that God was in change, not Pharaoh. But the magicians performed a similar trick and Pharaoh refused to believe in God or release the Israelites.

SHARE IT

▶ Who refuses to listen when you talk about Jesus?
▶ Do you pray for them regularly, and keep taking God's message to them?

PRAY ABOUT IT

Talk to God about people you know who refuse to accept the truth about Jesus. Ask Him to soften their hearts and to give you the strength and courage to keep talking to them.

➡ **TAKE IT FURTHER**

10 plagues for the price of 1 – p111.

14  Hopping mad

Pharaoh refused to let the Israelites go into the desert to worship God. The Lord turned all the water in Egypt to blood, but Pharaoh wouldn't give in. It's now a week later...

👁 Read Exodus 8 v 1–8

ENGAGE YOUR BRAIN

▶ What did Moses ask Pharaoh again? (v1)

▶ What was Pharaoh's surprise reply to the frog infestation? (v8)

The Egyptians worshipped many false gods. One of the popular ones was *Hekhet*, who was supposedly a woman with a frog's head. By sending the plagues, The Lord was showing that He was the one true God — the only one deserving worship.

Pharaoh was sick of frogs overrunning his palace, so he asked Moses and Aaron to ask God to get rid of them. In return, Pharaoh promised to let the Israelites worship God in the desert.

👁 Read verses 9–15

▶ Why did Moses tell Pharaoh to chose the time of the de-frogging? (v9–10)

▶ So what did Pharaoh do after God got rid of the frogs?

Moses let Pharaoh choose the time so no one could claim it was a coincidence when the frogs suddenly all died. It was obvious that God was behind it (v10). But as soon as the frogs left, Pharaoh hardened his heart and went back on his promise.

We can be just the same. In the middle of a crisis, we'll turn to God, begging Him to help us. Maybe even making promises to Him. But when the crisis is over and life gets back to normal, God is forgotten about and the promises are broken.

PRAY ABOUT IT

Ask God to help you talk to Him more often, not just when you need stuff. How can you start changing the way you pray RIGHT NOW?

➔ TAKE IT FURTHER

No *Take it further* today, so you'd best spend some more time in prayer.

17

15 : No flies on Moses

How good are you with bugs and flying things? How about if your house was infested with them — getting in your bed and landing on your cornflakes? How long before it would drive you mad?

👁 Read Exodus 8 v 16–19

ENGAGE YOUR BRAIN
▶ Could the magicians do a gnatty trick?

▶ What did they recognise about this plague?

Pharaoh's sorcerers couldn't conjure up a cloud of gnats, so they admitted that a power far greater than theirs must be in control. But, yet again, Pharaoh ignored the obvious and refused to listen.

👁 Read verses 20-32
▶ Why did God keep His people fly-free? (v22)

▶ What compromise did Pharaoh offer? (v25)

▶ Why wouldn't Moses accept the deal? (v26–27)

▶ Pharaoh's response this time? (v32)

Pharaoh tried to stay in control by offering to let the Israelites sacrifice to God... on his terms. Moses rightly stuck to his guns and said: 'God's way or no way'. Moses refused to compromise when it came to God's commands. Pharaoh gave in, but yet again changed his mind later.

God made a distinction between His people and His enemies — there were no flies on God's chosen people. Today, God's people are living under the same conditions as everyone else. But Christians are God's chosen people and one day will live in perfection with Him, far away from pain and misery and punishment.

PRAY ABOUT IT
Thank God that Christians are His chosen people and that, because of Jesus, He will separate them from sickness and misery and evil forever.

→ TAKE IT FURTHER
Follow the finger to page 111.

16 Boiling point

If you saw a sign that said: WARNING: VICIOUS BEASTS! would you just carry on strolling, ignoring it? Pharaoh kept ignoring God's painful warnings. Let's see how he does with warning number five.

👁 Read Exodus 9 v 1-7

ENGAGE YOUR BRAIN
- What distinction did God make between His people and the Egyptians? (v4, v7)

- Describe Pharaoh, in your own words:

God wasn't exactly being subtle. Pharaoh couldn't have missed the warnings. The Nile turned to blood; his palace was overrun with frogs, gnats and flies; and now all the livestock in Egypt dropped dead. But Pharaoh was stubborn and refused to acknowledge that God was all-powerful and in control.

👁 Read verses 8-12
- How did the magicians cope with this one?

- And Pharaoh? (v12)

The magicians had given up trying to copy A & M's miracles — they couldn't even stand up any more. But God made Pharaoh's heart hard, exactly as Pharaoh wanted it — and he refused to listen to God.

GET ON WITH IT
- How do you respond when God speaks to you through the Bible or at church?
- Do you take any notice?
- Do you listen to God and do what He says?

PRAY ABOUT IT
Pray for people you know who refuse to listen to warnings and keep their hearts closed to God. And ask the Lord to help you **listen** to Him and do what He commands.

THE BOTTOM LINE
Follow the warning signs.

➡ TAKE IT FURTHER
Pay day on page 111.

STUFF

Self-esteem

"Look in the mirror, go on, look at yourself. You're a tiger! What are you? I can't hear you... yeah! That's right! Say it: 'I'm a tiger'. Louder! You're a tiger! Let's hear you roar – grrr! You're a big, strong, confident tiger. Go out there and be a tiger today!"

TIGER OR MAGGOT?

Or perhaps you feel more like 'a maggot — a son of man, who is only a worm' (Job 25 v 6). We all have days when we feel pretty rubbish. Insignificant, stupid, ugly, unpopular. And if you're a Christian you can add feeling useless and sinful to the list. It's not a good place to be. But what's the answer? Do we need more positive thinking? To tell ourselves we're grrr-eat?

And what about days when everything's going right? — it's a good hair day; you came top in that test; everyone wants to be your mate; you've been asked to lead a Bible study at youth group because, hey, you're just so godly and humble... Does God think we're great too? Well, for both those sorts of days, the Bible has an answer. We're 'loved mud'. Sounds random? **Take a look at Psalm 103.**

MUDDY FEET

God made us — He knows we are dust, or mud (v14). On one hand that's literally true (Genesis 2 v 7), but it also shows how feeble we are. We sin (v3, 10, 12), we fail, and we get things wrong. If your best day were the brightest light bulb in the world, it would still look like a dark blob if you held it up against the sun. As 1 John 1 v 5 puts it: 'God is light; in him there is no darkness at all'. Get a sense of how far above us God is in verses 19–22 of Psalm 103.

LOVED MUD

We are mud. But we are loved mud. God forgives us (v3), He redeems us, rescuing us from the consequences of our sin (v4), and He gives us good

things (v5). Read verses 8-14 aloud to yourself.

HEART OF THE MATTER

Magazines, TV and friends would have us believe that image is everything — the way we look and the people we hang out with are all important. And if we don't live up to others' expectations, then we feel rotten. But God's view is very different: *'The Lord does not look at the things man looks at. Man looks at the outward appearance, but the Lord looks at the heart.'* (1 Samuel 16 v 7) The way we look is completely unimportant compared to what we're like on the inside — deep down are we living for ourselves or for God?

If we fear God — if we know he is in charge and try to live that way, His love will be with us for ever and ever (Psalm 103 v 17). It might not always feel that way, but if we want proof that we are loved, we just need to look at Psalm 103 v 10–12 again and then look back 2,000 years. God sent His Son to take our place. Jesus was punished for our sins. The ultimate sign of how highly God values us (check out amazing Romans 5 v 8).

PERMANENT LOVE

Our sense of self-worth shouldn't come from popularity, relationships or the way we look; it should come from knowing Jesus — His love for us will never fade or disappear. Our 'image' in this life is temporary, but God's love for His people is permanent.

God loves us, the mud that He made, enough to send Jesus to die for us. Not because 'you're worth it', but because of who He is: 'The LORD is compassionate and gracious, slow to anger, abounding in love' (v8).

So when you're looking in the bathroom mirror and you really don't feel like a tiger, remember that God loves you immensely. And one day, God will make all Christians perfect! And when you're tempted to think how grrr-eat you are, remember that you're also mud. Loved mud.

2 Timothy

Letter from death row

Rome, Italy. A beautiful city of stunning buildings on the gorgeous River Tiber. There's the Colosseum, the Forum and some great cafes. But in the year 66AD, Paul wasn't sight-seeing or sipping a cappuccino. He'd been chained up in prison by Emperor Nero, who hated Christians.

THE LAST WORD?

While on death row, Paul wrote another letter to his close friend Timothy. They had travelled across the Roman Empire together, spreading the gospel, for 15 years. Now Timothy was leading a church in Ephesus (in Turkey) and Paul was alone, expecting to die soon.

2 Timothy may have been the last letter Paul ever wrote — so what would the great apostle say? Would he make a will? Ask for another blanket? Beg for someone to get him out of jail?

SPREAD THE WORD

Well, the letter's got a number of touching personal requests, but they're just slipped in at the end. Paul had one overriding concern in the letter. He simply wanted to ensure the gospel of Jesus Christ would continue to spread once he was dead.

Paul wrote to urge Tim to stand up for the gospel. If the gospel was to survive after Paul's death, Tim needed to do two things: one, to carry on preaching it, and two, to train other people to preach it and spread it.

2 Timothy has some big lessons for us, encouraging us to stick with the gospel, to stand up for it and to be prepared to suffer for it. Paul says: 'Get stuck in!'

17

How would you describe yourself in just a few words? Shy, quiet bookworm? Loud, colourful basketball player? Cheerful, prayerful Christian? Go on, give it a go. Be honest.

👁 Read 2 Timothy 1 v 1–5

ENGAGE YOUR BRAIN
🔲 *How does Paul describe himself and then Timothy? (v1, v2, v5)*

Paul calls himself an *'apostle'* — someone sent out by God to tell people about Jesus. He's on death row but holding on to the promise of *'life with Christ Jesus'* — life here and now serving God, and eternal life with God once he's dead.

Paul feels fatherly towards younger Tim and this letter is packed full of wise advice. He also says that Tim has *'sincere faith'*, just as his mum and grandmother did (v5). And he has been constantly praying for Tim.

🔲 *How many people can you say you pray for constantly?*
🔲 *Do you need to change that?*

👁 Read verses 6–7
🔲 *What does Paul encourage Tim to do? (v6)*

🔲 *Why shouldn't Tim be timid when spreading the gospel?*

Paul says: *'Don't hold back and don't be shy — the Holy Spirit will help you serve God and spread the message.'* All Christians have the Holy Spirit helping them to powerfully tell people about Jesus; to show love to people around them; and to be self-disciplined, fighting sinful temptation.

SHARE IT
Yes, it can be terrifying to share your faith with people... BUT... we're not alone. God has given us the Spirit to help us live for Him and courageously share the gospel. God can easily overcome our lack of self-confidence!

PRAY ABOUT IT
1. Pray for other Christians you know.
2. Thank God for His Holy Spirit.
3. Ask Him to give you the courage to spread the gospel this week.

➡ TAKE IT FURTHER
Don't be shy, go over to page 112.

23

18 No shame

Is there anything you're ashamed of? Maybe embarrassed to let your dad talk to your friends? Or ashamed that you play the flute or collect stamps? But are you embarrassed about your faith?

👁 Read 2 Timothy 1 v 8–10

ENGAGE YOUR BRAIN

- ▶ *Why might Tim be ashamed of Paul or of the gospel?*
- ▶ *What did Paul ask Tim to do? (v8)*
- ▶ *What reasons did he give? (v9-10)*

In the first century AD, it was risky to preach about Jesus' death and resurrection. Paul was imprisoned for it and other Christians had been killed for preaching the gospel. Tim could easily have wimped out, but Paul called for Tim to suffer with him for the sake of the gospel.

And what great reasons he gives!
1) God has saved you.
2) He's called you to live a holy life.
3) You didn't deserve to be saved.
4) You're part of God's plans.
5) He's been so gracious to you.
6) God's plan to rescue sinners dates back to forever.
7) Jesus died and rose again to destroy death.
8) He's given you eternal life!

That's why we shouldn't be ashamed of the gospel, of Jesus or of being Christians. In fact, we should be prepared to suffer for spreading the incredible news of Jesus. Just look at what God has done for His people.

👁 Read verses 11–12

- ▶ *Why was Paul willing to suffer?*

Paul knows exactly why he's suffering. He knows that Jesus died in his place. And he's confident that one day he will live with Jesus eternally.

SHARE IT

- ▶ *How can those 8 reasons help you share the gospel?*
- ▶ *So, what will you do about it?*

PRAY ABOUT IT

Read v8–10, thanking God for all the things He's done for His people. Ask Him to help you not be ashamed of Him and His wonderful gospel.

➔ TAKE IT FURTHER

More on the gospel on page 112.

19 Right guard

Paul, the great gospel preacher, is in prison, facing death. He wants the gospel to keep spreading after he's gone, so he's writing to Tim, encouraging him to be brave; to stand up for the gospel; to suffer if necessary.

👁 Read 2 Timothy 1 v 13–14

ENGAGE YOUR BRAIN
▷ *If gospel truth was to survive, what two things was Tim to do?*

▷ *What help would he have? (v14)*

Tim should stick to the pattern of sound, life-giving teaching that he'd heard from Paul. Even when people around him were imprisoned or killed for preaching the gospel, Tim must hold on to the truth about Jesus — with **faith** in Jesus, showing **love** even to those who hassle him.

Tim must guard the truth of the gospel by making sure it's taught accurately and well. Thankfully, the Holy Spirit would help Him.

▷ *What does the gospel need guarding against these days?*

👁 Read verses 15–18
▷ *Who stuck by Paul through the hard times? (v16)*

▷ *How was he a shining example?*

Onesiphorus (he sounds like a dinosaur) was happy to be known as Paul's friend even though it was risky. He went to great lengths to find Paul in prison (v17) and helped him in loads of ways (v18).

GET ON WITH IT
▷ *How can you help Christians who are suffering for the gospel?*

▷ *Which Christian leaders can you help out? How?*

PRAY ABOUT IT
Thank God for giving the Holy Spirit to help believers hold on to the truth. And pray for Christians you know of who suffer for their faith.

THE BOTTOM LINE
Guard the gospel, support gospel-spreaders.

➔ TAKE IT FURTHER
Time to visit page 112.

20 ⌐ Pass it on ¬

Chinese whispers: whispering a phrase into someone's ear to pass it down the line. 'Don't be ashamed of the gospel' turns into 'Dopey Jamie's frogs smell'. Chinese whispers is what Paul DIDN'T want to happen to the gospel

👁 **Read 2 Timothy 2 v 1–2**

ENGAGE YOUR BRAIN

▶ What do you think v1 means?

▶ What's Tim to do with the gospel message?

Paul's advice to Tim is: 'Don't be ashamed of the gospel. Be strong. Rely on Jesus and what He's done for you — for forgiveness, power to keep going and hope for the future. And make sure you pass on what I taught you to people you trust to keep the truth of the gospel as they spread it.'

👁 **Read verses 3–7**

▶ What could Tim learn from...

a soldier? (v4)

an athlete? (v5)

a farmer? (v6)

The Christian life is tough. But Paul says be like a soldier; please your commanding officer — God. Don't get distracted from serving the Lord.

Athletes don't get gold medals if they cheat and take steroids. Paul says don't cut corners, don't just obey the Bible only when it suits you. You won't receive the prize of eternal life if you're faking it.

A farmer works his fingers to the bone to produce good crops. The Christian life is hard work. Stick at it, and you'll be rewarded. Eternally.

PRAY ABOUT IT
The Christian life is long, hard and involves suffering. But the rewards will be mind-blowing. Talk to God about the tough times. Ask Him for strength and perseverance. Thank Him for the great gift of eternal life.

➔ **TAKE IT FURTHER**
Pass the baton on page 112.

21 | To die for

Paul is so enthusiastic about the gospel — the truth about Jesus, His death and resurrection — he wants everyone to hear it and says it's even worth suffering for. Worth dying for.

👁 Read 2 Timothy 2 v 8–10

ENGAGE YOUR BRAIN

▶ What's at the heart of the gospel message? (v8)

▶ How is God's word different from prisoner Paul? (v9)

The core of the gospel message is Jesus — sent to the world as a man but raised from death to reign in heaven. Because of Jesus' death and resurrection, Paul was willing to 'endure everything' for teaching the incredible truth to 'the elect' — those God is going to save.

Paul could be chained up, but the gospel can't. God's word will continue to spread and transform lives.

👁 Read verses 11–13

▶ How do these verses show us that the gospel is worth suffering for?

▶ How do these words encourage people being persecuted?

This is probably an early Christian song. It's basically saying: *'Christians will suffer in this life, but God is faithful, so hold on for eternal life.'*

Christians no longer live for themselves: they now live for Christ and will live with Him forever (v11). Those who stick at it will one day rule with Him! (v12) But Jesus will turn His back on those who don't (v12).

PRAY ABOUT IT

Read through verses 8–13 slowly. What does it make you want to say to God? What do you need to say sorry for? What can you praise Him for?

THE BOTTOM LINE

Jesus is worth suffering for.

→ TAKE IT FURTHER

A little bit more on page 112.

22 | Unashamed workman

Paul's thoughts switched from his prison to the church where Tim was leader. Tim needed to be able to deal with false teachers in the church who were threatening the gospel and leading people away from Jesus.

👁 Read 2 Timothy 2 v 14–16

ENGAGE YOUR BRAIN

▶ What did Tim need to do in the church? (v14–16)

▶ With so much dodgy teaching around, why was it crucial that Tim did what v15 says?

Loads of top advice here. Most of it for church leaders, but there's plenty we can take to heart too.
• Don't fall out over things that don't matter so much.
• Make sure you're working for God and if you teach the Bible, make sure you get it right.
• Avoid ungodly talk; it will harm you.

GET ON WITH IT

▶ Which of these things do you need to deal with right now?

👁 Read verses 17–19

▶ What was the effect of this false teaching? (v18)

▶ Why won't such nonsense defeat the true gospel? (v19)

▶ What must Christians do? (v19)

The Bible says believers will rise from the dead and get new bodies when Jesus returns — that's what 'resurrection' means here (v18). But these false teachers claimed it had happened already. Rubbish.

Tim was struggling with false teachers in his church, but God knows which people are truly His. They show a desire to obey Him and turn away from wickedness (v19).

PRAY ABOUT IT

Pray through verses 14–16, talking to God about any of these things you need to deal with. Ask Him to help you stand firm and not be fooled by false teaching.

➔ TAKE IT FURTHER

More on the resurrection of the dead on page 113.

23

Run away!

Go open a random drawer in the kitchen. Which items in it are useful and which ones are useless? Why are you doing this??? Well, I thought you needed the exercise, but it also links in with today's 2 Tim talk.

👁 Read 2 Timothy 2 v 20–21

ENGAGE YOUR BRAIN
🖸 *What do you think Paul is waffling on about?*

What's with all this talk of kitchen drawers and household objects? Remember reading yesterday about Tim's trouble with false teachers? Well, they are like useless or *'ignoble'* items — God won't use them.

Instead, He seeks those who've been made holy, are useful to Him and are prepared to serve Him doing good stuff. Next, Paul mentions two things God's people must do.

👁 Read verse 22
🖸 *What are some of the 'evil desires of youth'?*

🖸 *What kind of things should Christians chase after?*

Strong words. We're not just told to ignore sinful desires, we must **sprint** away from them. If you find yourself in a tempting situation, get out of there; throw the DVD away; ditch those friends; block certain content on your PC; get yourself out of angry quarrels. Run away!

GET ON WITH IT
🖸 *What 'evil desires' do you need to run away from and kick out of your life?*

🖸 *What do you actually need to do to pursue righteousness, faith, love and peace?*

PRAY ABOUT IT
You know what you need to talk to God about today.

THE BOTTOM LINE
Flee sin, chase after holiness.

➔ TAKE IT FURTHER
Run away to page 113.

READING 2 Timothy 2 v 23–26

24 | Stupid squabbles

Ever had really heated arguments over pointless stuff?
I once had a fiery squabble with someone about whether
or not I was a cannibal! Ridiculous. Paul told Tim not to
get drawn into stupid arguments.

👁 Read 2 Timothy 2 v 23–24

ENGAGE YOUR BRAIN

- What exactly does Paul say about foolish arguments?
- What should God's servant do instead? (v24)

Silly little quarrels are not only a waste of time but they can turn into bigger disputes and get in the way of spreading the gospel. It's easy to get drawn into arguments, especially when we feel wronged. Paul says avoid fights, show kindness during arguments and don't hold grudges.

👁 Read verses 25–26

- How should Tim deal with people who oppose him?
- Why was it so important that Tim was gentle with such people?
- What was at stake? (v26)

Yes, Tim should fight for the truth — but gently. When people argue with us, we want to win them over to the gospel, not beat them in pointless

arguments. Getting fired up and aggressive won't help the gospel, but quietly opening your Bible with someone might.

Our arguments alone won't convince anyone to give their lives to Jesus — it's God who brings them to the truth (v25) so that they can escape the devil's clutches (v26).

GET ON WITH IT

- How can you act differently during disagreements?
- Who can you gently introduce to the truth about Jesus?

PRAY ABOUT IT

Ask God to help you conquer your anger and be gentle when people disagree with you. Ask Him to be working in the heart of the person you want to share the gospel with.

➡ TAKE IT FURTHER

More on the power of the gospel on page 113.

25

Terrible times

Paul is warning Tim about tough times ahead and false teachers spreading lies in the church. The 'last days' he mentions means the time between Jesus first coming and when He returns as Judge. That's right now.

👁 **Read 2 Timothy 3 v 1–5**

ENGAGE YOUR BRAIN

▶ *What are people like?*

▶ *Which of these things seem most relevant to our society?*

The beginning of v2 and the end of v4 sum up the whole list: **Lovers of themselves ... rather than lovers of God**. Putting yourself first before others leads to the other stuff — pride, boasting, abuse, disobedience to parents, lack of self-control and the rest. And God comes bottom of the list of priorities.

The really worrying bit is in v5 — many of these people call themselves believers! They go to church, say the right things, look the part but don't really live for God.

👁 **Read verses 6–9**

▶ *How are false teachers described? (v6–7)*

▶ *What will happen to them? (v8–9)*

Dodgy teachers claim to follow, but only love themselves. They prey on people who fall for their charms. Just like Pharaoh's magicians, Jannes and Jambres, who opposed Moses, they won't get far. People will soon see they have nothing genuine to offer.

PRAY ABOUT IT

Pray about people you know who refuse to put God first in their lives — maybe that's you. Pray for people you know who have been fooled by false religion, that God will open their eyes to the truth of Jesus.

THE BOTTOM LINE

Have nothing to do with false teachers.

➔ **TAKE IT FURTHER**

Grab some more on page 113.

26 | God's great Word

Most of us have older Christians we look up to — people who have had a big impact on our faith. For Timothy, it was Paul. He'd heard Paul preach the gospel and seen him suffer for it too.

Read 2 Timothy 3 v 10–13

ENGAGE YOUR BRAIN

How does Paul's life differ from the false teachers we've been reading about?

What's the tough promise for Christians? (v12)

Paul was a big influence on Tim's life. Tim could learn a lot from him — especially the way Paul was prepared to suffer for the gospel. That's the harsh reality of life as a Christian in a sinful world: we face persecution for our faith, while godless people go from bad to worse (v12–13).

Read verses 14–17

What was Tim to do and why? (v14–15)

Where does the Bible (Scripture) come from? (v16)

What should it be used for? (v16)

What's the great result? (v17)

This is how Christians can keep going despite persecution — living by God's Word. The Bible comes to us straight from God. As you read the Bible, God Himself is speaking to you: teaching you, disciplining you, setting you straight and training you in right living. Equipping you to serve Him.

GET ON WITH IT

How do you treat the Bible?

How can you make sure it impacts the way you live more?

PRAY ABOUT IT

Thank God for Christians who've had a big effect on your life. Pray for them. And ask God to help you take His Word more seriously and live by it.

THE BOTTOM LINE

All Scripture is God-breathed.

→ TAKE IT FURTHER

More on Paul's travels on page 113.

27 Fighting talk

Gospel heavyweight Paul took a hammering in his life. But he kept on fighting. And he wanted Tim to do the same.

👁 **Read 2 Timothy 4 v 1–5**

ENGAGE YOUR BRAIN

Paul's advice is particularly helpful to Christian leaders, but remember, 'All Scripture is God-breathed' so there's bound to be stuff for us too.

▶ *What were Tim's orders? (v2)*
▶ *Why should they be taken seriously? (v1)*
▶ *How should Tim respond to false teachers? (v5)*

This is serious stuff — that's why Paul mentions God's presence and reminds Tim that Jesus will one day return as Judge. Tim better take this seriously: Preach God's word! Be prepared! Correct false teaching! Encourage! Keep your head! Stick at it!

PRAY ABOUT IT

Pray for Christian leaders you know, that they will follow Paul's instructions and teach God's Word faithfully.

👁 **Read verses 6–8**

▶ *How was Paul a brilliant example to Tim? (v6–7)*
▶ *What's his prize?*

What an incredible description at the end of Paul's life. The hope of heaven and seeing Jesus face to face enabled him to keep fighting, keep sharing the gospel (even while in prison!) and to keep the faith. That should be our motivation too.

▶ *Do you long to see Jesus face to face?*
▶ *Why/why not?*

PRAY ABOUT IT

Thank God that Christians have the certain hope of eternal life with Him. Ask the Lord to help you stick at it, fighting for the gospel until your last breath.

THE BOTTOM LINE

Fight the good fight.

➔ TAKE IT FURTHER

Boxing clever on page 113.

33

28 | Getting personal

Paul is getting towards the end of his second letter to Timothy (I call it 'Tim: Book Two'). He's getting personal, with a few words about people Tim knows — some good, some bad.

👁 Read 2 Timothy 4 v 9–13

ENGAGE YOUR BRAIN

▶ How do you think Paul was feeling as he wrote this? (v9–11)

▶ Why did Demas desert Paul?

Paul was feeling lonely. Crescens, Titus and Tychicus (great names!) were on gospel missions and Demas had run out on Paul. LIke many people who seem to be following Christ, he was lured away from God by the temptations of the world. Only faithful Luke was still with Paul, so he asked that Tim and helpful Mark would join him before he died.

TALK IT THROUGH

▶ What kinds of things seduce people away from Christ?

▶ What steps can you take to avoid falling in love with the world?

▶ Who do you need to persuade to come back to living for God?

👁 Read verses 14–15

We need to watch out for people who oppose the gospel. We also need to watch our own reaction to them, making sure we don't become bitter and revengeful — we have to leave any punishment to God (v14).

PRAY ABOUT IT

1. Pray for people you know who 'love the world'.
2. Pray for Christians who are lonely.
3. Pray for Christians you know who quietly get on with serving God and other Christians.
4. Pray for people around you who hate Christianity.
5. Pray for yourself, that you won't be lured away by the temptations of the world.

➡ TAKE IT FURTHER

More strange names on page 114.

29 | Final words

We've reached the end of Paul's letter to Tim. It's been packed with teaching, warning and encouragement to keep spreading the gospel, whatever it costs.

👁 **Read 2 Timothy 4 v 16**

ENGAGE YOUR BRAIN

▶ *What was Paul's attitude towards those who'd deserted him?*

▶ *How do you react when people let you down?*

Paul had been in court, accused by the Romans who wanted him dead. No one had showed up to support him, yet Paul didn't hold it against them. Amazing. It's so easy to hold grudges against people who let us down, but Paul encourages us to follow his example!

▶ *Who do you need to forgive and treat better? (v17)*

👁 **Read verses 17–22**

▶ *What was the great news when Paul was alone?*

▶ *What did God enable him to do? (v17)*

▶ *What could Paul be confident of?*

None of Paul's friends had been with him, but the Lord was at his side, giving him the strength he needed to shout the truth about Jesus (v17).

He was completely confident that God would rescue him and keep him safe. Not necessarily physically, as Paul knew he might be killed for preaching about Jesus. But God would keep him safe *eternally*, bringing him safely to His eternal kingdom. Awesome stuff.

PRAY ABOUT IT

Verse 18 is true for all believers. Read it (out loud if you can) and praise God for its incredible truth.

THE BOTTOM LINE

Christians are safe with the Lord. Eternally.

➜ TAKE IT FURTHER

More on page 114.

Killed for Christ

Each month in REAL LIVES, we bring you stories of people whose lives have been transformed by Christ. This issue, we dive into the history books for the extraordinary story of William Hunter.

TRAGIC DEATH

William Hunter was a young man from Brentwood, Essex, England. He was burned alive at the age of 19 because of his Christian faith. It was March 1555, a time when it wasn't safe to be a Bible-believer in England. The Catholic queen, Mary I, was on the throne and was doing everything in her power to stamp out the Reformation. (Don't know what the Reformation is? Look it up on Wikipedia or ask someone at church.) William was the first martyr in Essex, one of almost three hundred Christians burned to death across the country. Horrific.

BUSTED FOR BIBLE READING

The trouble began when William was caught reading the Bible in a chapel in Brentwood. The local vicar, Thomas Wood, told him he had no right to *'meddle with the Scriptures'* and had William arrested. He was taken down to London for interrogation, where he testified that he trusted in Christ alone for salvation and would not stop reading the Bible.

At first, the Bishop of London (the judge in the case) promised to set William free if only he would give up his reformation beliefs. Next the bishop promised him £40 (a large amount in those days) to set up his own business but William refused to change his mind. When William was offered bribes by the bishop he replied: *'I thank you for your great offers, my Lord, but if you cannot persuade me from the Scriptures, I cannot turn from God for love of the world. I count all worldly*

As the flames rose around him, he cried: 'Lord, receive my spirit'.

things as loss and dung compared to the love of Christ.' In other words, he knew that there's nothing more precious in life than friendship with Jesus Christ — and he wouldn't give that up for anything in the world.

BURNED ALIVE

So they took him back to Brentwood for execution in the fire — a gruesome way to die. Even as he was being chained to the stake, he was offered a last-minute reprieve. The sheriff produced an official-looking document and announced: _'Here is a letter from the Queen. If you recant,_ (deny your beliefs) _you shall live; if not, you shall be burned.'_ As the flames rose around him, he lifted his hands to heaven and cried: _'Lord, Lord, Lord, receive my spirit'_, before being smothered by the smoke.

SO WHAT?

There are many lessons we can learn from William Hunter. One challenge is his deep passion for the Bible. In Brentwood, near the place where he was martyred, there's a memorial which reads: _'Christian reader, learn from his example to value the privilege of an open Bible and be careful to maintain it.'_ William was hungry for God's Word. Right now there are more Bibles in circulation than ever before, but where is our passion for God's Word? Why aren't we hungry to read the Bible, to learn from the Word of God?

A second way in which William challenges us is by his passion for eternity. He wanted to live life with a heavenly perspective. Among his last words on the day before his death, he reassured his mother: _'For the little pain I shall suffer, which shall soon end, Christ has promised me a crown of joy.'_ William was focused on eternity. He wasn't chasing wealth and comfort, but wanted most of all to glorify Jesus whatever it took — even if that meant losing his life for the sake of the gospel. We need to recapture that eternal heavenly perspective, because it will transform the way we live here on earth.

Taken from an interview with Andrew Atherstone — tutor in history at Wycliffe Hall, Oxford. For more stories of the Reformation martyrs, see his book The Martyrs of Mary Tudor (Day One, available from Christian bookshops).

30 | Bombarded by brilliance

As the prisoner flees across the yard, the security system is triggered. Nothing escapes the glare of the floodlights and he's exposed — no cover, no excuses, he makes himself as small as possible....

Keep that picture in mind as you...

👁 Read Psalm 19 v 1–6

ENGAGE YOUR BRAIN

▶ *The sky has a message. What is it?*

▶ *Where and when can it be heard?*

THINK IT OVER

Do you know anyone who's dismissed faith in God due to a lack of evidence? According to David, they're just not listening. We're living under a permanent, international demonstration of the wonder of God. Just look around you!

👁 Read verses 7–14

▶ *Write down the descriptions of God's commands and words.*

▶ *Faced with such perfection, what two types of sin does David become aware of? (v 12–13)*

Not only does the sun beat down a daily reminder of God's power, He's given us His perfect and precious commands. What can match the insight and plain-talking truth of the Bible? Quite simply, everything that comes from God is beyond brilliant.

PRAY ABOUT IT

As you come face to face with the God of obvious power and unbeatable wisdom, make v14 the words of your own prayer.

GET ON WITH IT

Find five minutes today to spend with Psalm 19 in the open air. Don't forget to look up!

→ TAKE IT FURTHER

Listen to the voices and go to page 114.

31 Winning mentality

It's great for a sports team to expect victory and be full of confidence. It's another thing all together to advance-order crates of champagne and an open-top bus for the victory parade. Just how confident should a Christian be?

Read Psalm 20 v 1–5

ENGAGE YOUR BRAIN

David has composed a prayer to be used when the nation's on the brink of war.

▷ What help and protection can they expect? (v1–2)

▷ What scene are they imagining when it's all over? (v5)

THINK IT OVER

Approaching a tough challenge, you can find your knees shaking. Knowing you're backed up by a huge bank balance, crowds of fans and years of experience can add a sense of security — but what if you've nothing on your side but God?

Read verses 6–9

▷ What's the result of trusting in military might? (v7–8)

▷ What's the result of depending on God?

Bold words. But what makes David so sure that faith works? Check out 1 Samuel 17 v 45–47.

If David is a sneak preview, Jesus is the real thing — the anointed King! Since His epic battle with the enemy is now past, the cross and resurrection history, the result is guaranteed; we can be ultra confident of the coming victory celebration.

THE BOTTOM LINE

Some trust in _____
and _____ but
we trust in the name of our God.
Fill in the blanks with popular alternatives to God-focused living.

PRAY ABOUT IT

Admit to God about times when you rely on yourself and not Him. Then pray — tell Him everything: don't hold back, and ask Him to help you trust Him more.

→ TAKE IT FURTHER

Jesus' winning way — page 115.

32

The secret of success

It's time to collect your Oscar. Having dressed up like royalty, walked the red carpet and wrestled the paparazzi, you step up to receive your reward. As you tentatively approach the microphone, who will you thank?

👁 Read Psalm 21 v 1–13

ENGAGE YOUR BRAIN
Compare the king's victory song (v1–7) with the fate of his enemies (v8–12).

▶ Who gets what they want? (v2, v11)

▶ What is their destiny? (v4, v10)

▶ What will they get when they meet God? (v6, v9)

THINK IT OVER
But why is God on the king's side? Because he's all about God's glory (v1). These are God's military campaigns fought with heaven's muscle. (See what happens with David's own hairbrained scheme in 1 Chronicles 21 v 13–14)

👁 Read Psalm 21 v 4–7
▶ Why might his hopes in v4 and v6 sound like an exaggeration?

With his feet still rooted to the earth, David's speaking as if he's in heaven already — it sounds a bit odd. But try putting these words in the mouth of Jesus. They fit perfectly. Jesus is the everlasting king, and here we get a snapshot of His passion and purpose. (More of this in the next psalm.)

GET ON WITH IT
The point of life is not to big yourself up, but to show that Jesus is the best. Get a sticky note, and write on it the goal of your existence, in your own words. Attach it to the ceiling, above your bed, or whatever is the first thing you see each day.

PRAY ABOUT IT
In John 17 v 20–23, Jesus prays for us! Read it and put yourself in the picture. Ask God that together with your church, youth group or Christian mates, you'll find ways to let the world know of His outrageous love.

➔ TAKE IT FURTHER
Great stuff on page 115.

33 | Heartcry of a hero

Some songs sound familiar. Perhaps they're just so cleverly crafted that you feel as if you've heard them before... or maybe the lyrics and tune have actually been stolen from another song.

👁 **Read Psalm 22 v 1–21**

ENGAGE YOUR BRAIN

ⅅ *Find the verses that sound like quotes from Jesus' crucifixion.*

ⅅ *His cry from the cross:*

ⅅ *Mocked by soldiers:*

ⅅ *Gambling for His robe:*

ⅅ *The nails:*

(All these details also feature in Mark 15 v 16–39.)

THINK IT OVER

This is no freaky coincidence. According to Hebrews 2 v 12, we can hear the words of Psalm 22 as Jesus' own. It's mind-boggling that this song, so clearly telling us about Jesus' last hours, was composed hundreds of years before!

👁 **Read verses 22–31**

ⅅ *What will He be doing? (v22, v25)*

ⅅ *What does He call us to do? (v23–24)*

ⅅ *What will be the world's response now and in the future? (v30–31)*

This psalm is like reading an 'interview' with the Saviour of the entire world, even as the rescue takes place! It reveals that through excruciating agony and humiliation, Jesus saw the bigger picture — God being massively honoured as future generations hear His message of ultimate love. As He died, you were on His mind.

PRAY ABOUT IT

Now re-read v22–31, and join in worshipping the God who gave His Son for you.

→ TAKE IT FURTHER

Keep on going to page 115.

34

Off course?

The GPS/sat nav takes you down a country lane at night. As the tarmac becomes a dirt track, you start to doubt the voice of technology. But how do you know you're on the right track with God?

👁 **Read Psalm 23 v 1–3**

ENGAGE YOUR BRAIN

▶ How is the Shepherd's route described? (v3)

▶ Why does He lead David along the right path? (v3)

THINK IT OVER

It might seem surprising that God's main concern in leading David is His own reputation. But then again, since the focus of the entire universe is the fame of heaven's King (look back at Psalm 19), steering our lives in the same direction is a smart choice.
If we're being shepherded for God's purposes, what can go wrong?
'If God is for us, who can be against us?' (Romans 8 v 31)

👁 **Read verses 4–6**

▶ How does David feel during dark times? (v4)

▶ Who's watching at the feast? (v5)

Just because the path is set by God doesn't make it easy. But even in the darkest place, God's supplies are limitless.

THINK IT OVER

▶ What's the worst thing you can imagine happening to you?

Painful as it is, picture it. Can God's love reach you there? Absolutely.

THE BOTTOM LINE

Make it your goal to trust the presence and love of God to take you through great times and hard times.

GET ON WITH IT

Add Habakkuk 3 v 17–18 to your bedroom décor. Adopt it as a defining attitude for life, especially during tough times.

➡ **TAKE IT FURTHER**

On the road again... page 116.

35 | Red carpet treatment

As Brad Pitt arrived for a Film Festival, a crazed woman dived towards him. The crowd gasped. Thankfully, she only wanted a hug. How far would you go to meet a superstar?

👁 Read Psalm 24 v 1–10

ENGAGE YOUR BRAIN

Psalm 24 introduces God as the planet's founder and landlord.

▶ *What kind of person is fit for a close encounter with Him? (v3–4)*

Verses 7–10 could be describing the excitement when the ark of the covenant was brought to Jerusalem. The ark (not the boat, more like a treasure chest) was a symbol of God's presence and blessing. If God was moving in, no wonder they wanted to get the doors wide open!

👁 Read verses 7–10 again

▶ *List the words that accompany 'King' and 'Lord' to describe God.*

▶ *What can stand in the way of someone like that?*

THINK IT OVER

In the New Testament, God's people, are called *'the temple'* (2 Corinthians 6 v 16–18). If God's at home in us, He's calling us to live clean lives, devoted to purity.

PRAY ABOUT IT

Yourself

▶ *How do your heart (attitudes) and hands (actions) need a good scrub?*

Your church

▶ *How might it need styling less like the world and more like God?*

Thank God that, though we're a work in progress, He longs to bless and forgive those seeking Him (v5–6).

➔ TAKE IT FURTHER

Walk down the red carpet to page 116.

ESSENTIAL

That's the Spirit

In each issue of **engage** we'll take time out to explore a key truth about God, the Bible and Christianity. In ESSENTIAL we gather together the teaching from the Bible on a particular subject, and try to explain it. This issue, we're looking at the Holy Spirit.

It's a simple fact. By ourselves, we're completely useless.

We can't make ourselves Christians. We can't make ourselves better people. We can't serve God in the way He wants us to. Not by ourselves. But all these things are possible through the third person of the Trinity... the Holy Spirit (AKA the *Holy Ghost*, *Spirit of God*, *Spirit of Jesus*, or just *the Spirit*).

WHO IS THE HOLY SPIRIT?

He's God. The third person of the Trinity along with the Father and the Son. Not a force. Not an 'it'. He's God and has been around since before the beginning of time. In the Old Testament we find Him doing things like assisting with creation (Psalm 104 v 30), and giving important people like the prophets and kings the wisdom they need to say and do what God wants (Isaiah 61 v 1). But in the New Testament, from Pentecost onwards (Acts 2), the Spirit is poured out into the lives of everyone who believes in Jesus.

WHAT DOES HE DO?

Jesus tells us that the Spirit is given to be our *'Counsellor'* or helper (John 14 v 16–17). So how does He help us?

1. Helps us understand the gospel

It's the Holy Spirit who helps us understand we're sinners (John 16 v 5–11); helps us see that Jesus is the bringer of forgiveness and the only way to God (John 16 v 12–15); helps us understand the things Jesus did and Jesus said (John 14 v 26). When

to be a Christian (Romans 8 v 16–21) and keep our eyes fixed on the exciting future that waits for us in eternity (Ephesians 1 v 13–14). He even helps us pray when we find that hard! (Romans 8 v 26)

3. Helps us spread the gospel

The Spirit wants us to understand how brilliant Jesus is. So He stirs up believers to tell others about Christ. Every Christian is a useful member of God's family. Each one of us has a job to do for the Lord. You may be someone who teaches others the Bible or just take cakes round to a little old lady. But whatever the job is, it's a vital part of the great, world-wide plan to help other people come to faith in Jesus and grow in their faith. The Holy Spirit helps by giving every Christian 'gifts' — talents that will help us serve God in His exciting work in the world. (Romans 12 v 6–8; 1 Corinthians chapter 12).

we become a Christian, the Holy Spirit is with us enabling us to take that step of commitment. When we read the Bible, He's working in our lives, ensuring that we understand God's words to us. When we listen to Christian talks, He's working away to make sure we get what the speaker is saying. The most incredible truth is that *everyone* who is a real Christian has God's Spirit living inside them (Romans 8 v 9).

2. Helps us become more like Jesus

But being a Christian isn't about understanding facts, it's about living our life God's way. The Holy Spirit enables us to battle temptation and become more like Jesus. When the Spirit is changing us, we can (over time) become radically different people (Galatians 5 v 19–25). He helps us keep going when it's tough

4. He helps us work together

The Spirit stirs up Christians' love for each other, so that we have 'fellowship' — the experience of belonging, working together and supporting each other. And He builds us into a people — a universal church united in Jesus — who love believing, living and serving together as a family.

Want to know more? Spend time looking up the Bible bits we've mentioned and the Holy Spirit will teach you more about Him and His amazing work in our lives.

John

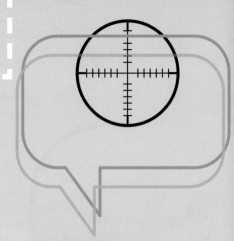

Famous last words

AND FINALLY...

Jesus' last words on earth were not flippant or foolish. They were words of prayer, truth, obedience, hope and peace. As we read the last few chapters of John's Gospel, we'll listen in as Jesus prays for His disciples, faces His accusers, obeys His Father all the way to death, and then speaks of forgiveness and peace after rising from the dead.

But there are not just words here.

READING THE SIGNS

As John narrates the events of Jesus' last few days on earth, we see the biggest sign of all. Bigger than water into wine, bigger than the feeding of the 5,000. Jesus' last sign is His death and resurrection — the biggest signpost of all.

And what's it pointing to? Eternal life.

Check out John 20 v 30–31:

Jesus did many other miraculous signs in the presence of his disciples, which are not recorded in this book. But these are written that you may believe that Jesus is the Christ, the Son of God, and that by believing you may have life in his name.

Let's throw ourselves into the final chapters of this amazing book. Listen out for Jesus' famous last words and look out for the signs.

36 The time has come

The whole of chapter 17 is a prayer by Jesus. We get to listen in and discover what He thinks is important for Himself and His followers, as He prepares to face death on the cross and return to His Father.

👁 Read John 17 v 1–5

ENGAGE YOUR BRAIN

🔽 Who is Jesus praying for in these verses?

🔽 Why is He praying? (v1)

Remember *'the hour'* or *'the time'* from earlier in John's Gospel? It referred to the most important event in history — the time when Jesus would die. Jesus' purpose and mission was clear from the beginning. He was always heading for the cross.

🔽 What is Jesus asking His Father for? (v1 and v5)

🔽 Why does He deserve it?

Stop and think for a minute about how glorious Jesus really is.

🔽 What is the definition of eternal life according to v3?

SHARE IT

Have you realised that if you're a Christian then you have already started living forever? Knowing the only true God and His Son Jesus personally is the beginning of eternal life. Do your friends really get what eternal life is all about? Not harps and clouds after death but an ongoing relationship with the Creator and Saviour of the world. Can you explain that to someone today?

PRAY ABOUT IT

Thank God that we can know Him because Jesus has shown us what God is like. Thank Him that we can have a relationship with Him because Jesus died instead of us. Pray for people you know who don't yet know Him. Ask Him to help you point them to Jesus.

THE BOTTOM LINE

Jesus deserves all the glory.

➔ TAKE IT FURTHER

The time has come to turn to p.117.

37 Faithful followers

Now Jesus turns to praying for his disciples, who had followed him for three years. Let's take a close look at what He says about them.

👁 **Read John 17 v 6–10**

ENGAGE YOUR BRAIN

▶ *Can you sum up the disciples under these three headings?*

What God did (v6, 7, 8 & 9):

What Jesus did (v6 & 8);

What the disciples did (v6–10):

We can see here one of the wonderful truths about the way God works — He gave people to Jesus to be His but they also believed and chose to follow and obey Jesus. God is in charge but human beings are responsible for their actions it's a bit mind boggling but both are true.

TALK IT OVER

How is that truth a big encouragement when we think about sharing Jesus with our non-Christian friends? Really think it through with an older Christian. How does it stop us feeling under pressure to convert people? How does it stop us sitting back and not bothering to talk about Christ?

PRAY ABOUT IT

Thank God that He chose you. Thank Him that you belong to Him forever and ever.

THE BOTTOM LINE

Jesus is glorified when people believe in Him.

➡ **TAKE IT FURTHER**
A little more on page 117.

38 Facing foes

As Jesus looked ahead, He knew He wouldn't be physically with His disciples for much longer. They were about to face some testing times, so what does He pray for them?

👁 Read John 17 v 11-19

ENGAGE YOUR BRAIN

▶ *What danger do the disciples face? (v11, v15)*

▶ *Why is this the case? (v14)*

Jesus kept the disciples safe while He was on earth (except Judas who betrayed Jesus — v12), but He knows they will face the same opposition He did so He prays for God's protection over them.

▶ *What else does Jesus pray for the disciples (v11, v17)?*

To be sanctified is to be set apart, holy, devoted to God, shaped by His word, His truth.

Notice what Jesus says in verse 15? Being set apart for God doesn't mean hiding in a monastery or nunnery praying all day; it means living all out for God wherever you are at the moment.

GET ON WITH IT

Disciples of Jesus are to be:
a) in the world, but set apart for God to use in the world
b) not compromising in obeying Jesus
c) not detached from the world, living in a Christian bubble.

▶ *a) Are you actually letting God's truth change you?*
▶ *b) In what areas have you stopped obeying Jesus?*
▶ *c) How can you have more contact with non-Christians?*

PRAY ABOUT IT

See how Jesus addresses God in v11? *'Holy Father'* — God is awesomely holy and perfect, but He is also our loving Father. Remember both of these things as you talk to Him now about what you've learnt.

THE BOTTOM LINE

God keeps us safe and holy.

➡ TAKE IT FURTHER

Out of this world — page 117.

39 Faith in the future

Who does Jesus focus His prayer on next? Take a look in the mirror. Yes, He prayed for you — even before you were born. Amazing.

👁 **Read John 17 v 20–23**

ENGAGE YOUR BRAIN

Take a look at v20. If you believe the message about Jesus that the disciples passed on, written down in the Bible, then this prayer is for you!

▶ *What does Jesus want for His followers (including you and me)?*

▶ *Why? (v21b, v23)*

There's a lot of talk about unity in the church and, to be honest, there doesn't often seem to be much unity at all. But look at the sort of unity Jesus is talking about — as we are united to Jesus and His Father by believing and trusting in Christ (v20), He will be just as close to us as He is to His Father.

It's a bit like a bicycle wheel: Jesus is the hub and individual Christians are the spokes — the closer we are to Jesus, the closer we become to each other.

▶ *Why do you think true Christian unity is such a powerful witness to the rest of the world?*

TALK IT OVER

Unity at any cost? What are the limits (if any) of Christian unity? What do we need to agree on and what can we agree to differ on? Think it through with a Christian friend.

PRAY ABOUT IT

Pray for your church and/or youth group — that the Christians there will be united in love for each other in serving God together.

➡ **TAKE IT FURTHER**

United we stand... on page 117.

40 | Final frontier

As He finishes His prayer, Jesus looks even further into the future. His focus is on eternity and it still includes you and me!

👁 **Read John 17 v 24–26**

ENGAGE YOUR BRAIN

🔘 *How does Jesus describe His relationship with His father (v24)?*

🔘 *Where does Jesus want His followers to be (v24)?*

When Jesus says *'I want'* in v24, He's not just expressing a preference. It's more like *'I will that'* — it is going to happen.

Stop for a minute and think about how awesome it is that Christians are headed for this future.

🔘 *Do we deserve it?*

🔘 *So what makes it possible for us to share in that?*

🔘 *What else does Jesus want His followers to have? (v26)*

🔘 *What do we already know about this love? (v24)*

You might find it hard to get your head around the Trinity (who doesn't?!) but at the heart of God is an eternally loving relationship, and He wants us to be part of that. Amazing.

PRAY ABOUT IT

Talk to God now about your response to that truth. Thank Him that knowing Jesus means you are headed for a perfect eternity of love.

THE BOTTOM LINE

Christians are headed for an eternity of perfect love with God.

→ TAKE IT FURTHER

Not so mushy love on page 117.

41　Time for arrest

Time's up. The hour is here and everything goes according to plan. God's plan, that is. What happens to Jesus is awful but at the same time totally under control. Let's take a look...

👁 Read John 18 v 1–14

ENGAGE YOUR BRAIN

▶ What do we learn about the olive grove? (v2)

▶ What does that tell us about Jesus? And Judas?

▶ What does v4 tell us about Jesus?

▶ What does Jesus say about Himself? (v5–8)

▶ How do His enemies respond?

By saying 'I am he' or more specifically 'I am', Jesus was echoing the name God gave to Himself in the Old Testament (Exodus 3 v 13–15).

▶ See how Jesus' prayer from the last chapter is answered already? (v8-9)

▶ Why was Peter's action in v11 brave but stupid?

The cup that Jesus mentions is a symbolic way of talking about God's anger and judgment.

▶ What does John point out that is significant about Caiaphas?

PRAY ABOUT IT
Back in 11 v 50 the same Caiaphas said: 'It is better … that one man die for the people than that the whole nation perish'. He was trying to avoid trouble with the Romans, but ironically what he said was true — that is exactly what happened on the cross when one man gave His life to pay for the sins of many.

PRAY ABOUT IT
Talk to God about how you feel as you read these verses.

→ TAKE IT FURTHER
Fancy a cuppa? Try page 117.

42   Out in the cold

One minute Peter's making extravagant promises (13 v 37) and waving his sword around (18 v 10). The next... well, it's a pretty sorry story.

👁 Read John 18 v 15–18

ENGAGE YOUR BRAIN
▶ *What's promising about v15–16?*

▶ *If you didn't know the rest of the story, what might you expect Peter and John to do next?*

▶ *How does it all go wrong?*

The girl on duty at the gate was probably a servant and about as low down the pecking order as you could get. Certainly not a threat to Peter — she didn't even have a weapon like Malchus and the soldiers.

▶ *What's so tragic about Peter's words? (v17)*

▶ *Why do you think he had changed so much since v10?*

When it came down to it, Peter didn't want to stick out. He huddled round the fire like everyone else, and tried to blend in. All his bravado faded away.

PRAY ABOUT IT
Be honest. Are you ever tempted to act like Peter? To keep your head down and pretend that you've got nothing to do with Jesus? Or to make big claims about your faith that you don't live up to? Say sorry to God now and ask for His help to change.

THE BOTTOM LINE
When it comes to standing up for Jesus, we're often weak. We need God's strength.

→ TAKE IT FURTHER
Follow Peter to page 117.

53

43 | Trial and error

From this point on things just get worse for Jesus —
a corrupt trial, a cowardly judge and desertion by His
closest friends. But Jesus is ready for it all.

👁 Read John 18 v 19–24

ENGAGE YOUR BRAIN

▶ What two things does Annas
want to find out from Jesus?
(v19)

▶ What is Jesus' answer?

Although Caiaphas was the actual
high priest, Annas had held the
position before him so was probably
still considered a religious bigwig
by the Jewish people. They still end
up taking Jesus to see Caiaphas
afterwards, but it's a mockery of a
trial. Not fair, not legal.

▶ What is missing from this 'trial'?
(v21)

▶ How do Jesus' enemies respond?
Is this fair? (v22)

▶ What is different about the way
Jesus behaves? (v23)

Jesus is open and honest; His accusers
are secretive (holding his 'trial' at
night), biased and illegal. This huge
contrast simply highlights what
needed to happen at the cross —
a perfect sacrifice dying for sinful
people.

PRAY ABOUT IT

Spend some time admitting your
own sin before God. Thank Him for
sending Jesus to take the punishment
you deserve for all that sin.

THE BOTTOM LINE

Remember Jesus' words — He is the
way, the truth and the life.

→ TAKE IT FURTHER

Trial offer... on page 118.

Stand up or let down

Peter didn't need to be so worried — despite being quizzed about His disciples, Jesus has kept the attention firmly on Himself and His teaching. But for poor Peter things keep getting worse.

👁 Read John 18 v 25–27

ENGAGE YOUR BRAIN

▶ How does Peter's behaviour compare with Jesus' in the previous verses?

▶ What evidence is Peter faced with? (v26)

▶ What is his response?

👁 Read John 13 v 37–38

Jesus knew Peter would let Him down, even when Peter made all sorts of claims about his loyalty. God knows our weaknesses and He is gracious towards us. Even though Peter has fallen so far, there is hope of forgiveness for Him — wait till we get to chapter 21.

THINK IT THROUGH

It's easy to be critical of Peter for turning his back on Jesus, but be honest as you answer these questions:

▶ Have you ever said you did 'nothing much' on Sunday?

▶ Ever kept quiet while people poked fun at Jesus?

▶ Have you felt too embarrassed to tell friends you're a Christian?

▶ Chickened out of saying you believe what the Bible says?

Are you still critical of Peter or can you identify with him?

PRAY ABOUT IT

Read Psalm 103 and use it as a starting point for your own prayer.

THE BOTTOM LINE

God knows our weaknesses.

→ TAKE IT FURTHER

No Take It Further today. Sorry!

45 Plots and plans

The action moves to Pilate's Roman palace now, where Jesus faces more corruption. The Jewish leaders hate Jesus so much they're willing to team up with their Roman enemies to get rid of Him.

👁 Read John 18 v 28

ENGAGE YOUR BRAIN

▶ *What is so hypocritical about the Jews' attitude in v28?*

'Oooh, let's not go into that nasty Roman palace, we don't want to be ceremonially unclean — God wouldn't like that!' Executing an innocent man unjustly? *'Oh that's fine! I'm sure God won't mind that.'*

There's a bit of an argument between Pilate and the Jewish leaders next.

👁 Read verses 29–32

▶ *How would you sum up their relationship?*

▶ *What do the Jews want from Pilate?*

For all their influence and corrupt court proceedings, the Jews didn't have the power of execution — their Roman bosses had that. Even though sometimes they were allowed to stone people to death, the Jews wanted a proper Roman execution — a crucifixion.

See v32? Jesus always knew what sort of death He would be facing.

SHARE IT

Why did Jesus have to die? Because He was a political revolutionary? Because He was ahead of His time? Because His enemies were too smart for Him? Or because it was part of God's plan? Ask your friends what they think, then try to explain what the Bible teaches about it all.

THE BOTTOM LINE

God's plans are much bigger than human scheming and corruption.

➔ TAKE IT FURTHER

Why crucifixion? Try page 118.

46

The truth is out there

Jesus now faces more questioning, this time from Pilate.
Unlike the Jewish leaders, he's not out for Jesus' blood.
Sadly, he's not interested in justice either.

👁 Read John 18 v 33–40

ENGAGE YOUR BRAIN

▶ What is Jesus charged with?
(v33-35)

▶ Why would this have been a
threat to the Romans?

▶ Does Pilate find Jesus guilty of
this charge? (v38)

▶ What offer does he make the
Jews? (v39)

Barabbas was an anti-Roman terrorist,
a convicted murderer. And they want
him freed instead of Jesus? A guilty
man set free and an innocent man
executed? Remind you of anything?

PRAY ABOUT IT

Thank God for that amazing swap —
that we can be free instead of being
punished as our sins deserve.

The irony is that the accusation Jesus
faced was true — well, half true.
Jesus is a king, not just of the Jews
but of the whole world. But Pilate
can't get his head round the sort of
king that Jesus is; not political but
heavenly (v36).

▶ What is the challenge Jesus lays
before Pilate? (v37)

▶ What does Pilate's response tell
us about the sort of person he is?

TALK IT OVER

Why do you think people find it so
hard to accept that 'the truth is out
there' — in Jesus Christ? Chat about
it with another Christian, maybe
looking at Romans 1 v 18–32.

THE BOTTOM LINE

Jesus is the King of kings.

→ TAKE IT FURTHER

The hard truth is on page 118.

47 Terrible torture

Although Pilate has already said that he doesn't think Jesus is guilty, he doesn't set Him free either. Let's see what God's King had to face on His way to the cross.

👁 Read John 19 v 1–5

ENGAGE YOUR BRAIN

▶ *What do you think Pilate hoped to achieve by having Jesus flogged?*

▶ *Why are verses 2–3 so awful?*

▶ *What is Pilate's verdict on Jesus?*

▶ *How many times does he say this between 18 v 38 – 19 v 6?*

▶ *What point does that make?*

▶ *Does Jesus really look like a threat to the Romans in v5?*

The Ruler of the universe, insulted, mocked and beaten. It makes you feel sick to think about it. But where would you have been 2,000 years ago? There's a song that goes: *'Behold the man upon the cross, my sin upon his shoulders; Ashamed, I hear my mocking voice, call out among the scoffers'.*

PRAY ABOUT IT

Jesus went to the cross for the sins of the world — including yours. Think about that. Talk to Him about it.

THE BOTTOM LINE

Jesus the King, suffered for sinners.

➔ TAKE IT FURTHER

For an awesome description of all-powerful King Jesus, turn to page 118.

48 Death sentence

More pathetic arguing between Pilate and the Jews as they try to push the responsibility for killing Jesus onto one another. Despite all of their pointless back and forth, it is clear that God is ultimately in control of events.

Read John 19 v 6–16

ENGAGE YOUR BRAIN

- What is the attitude of the chief priests and officials in v6?
- What is Pilate's response?
- Why do the Jews really hate Jesus? (v7)
- What is Pilate's response this time?
- What does he need to realise about his authority? (v11)
- What does that tell us about all these events?
- Look carefully again at v11. Is Pilate blameless? How about Caiaphas?

It's that key truth again. God is in control, but human beings are equally responsible for their actions. Pilate and Caiaphas and the rest are guilty of putting an innocent man to death, but amazingly God uses their schemes to bring about His own plan to save the world.

PRAY ABOUT IT

Thank God that His plans cannot be frustrated or stopped by evil.

- How do the Jews bully Pilate into doing what they want (v12)?
- Who are they ultimately rejecting by their claim in v15?

Perhaps they were claiming to be loyal to Caesar and Rome, but in actual fact they were rejecting God — who was always the true King of Israel. Shocking stuff, but that's exactly what we do if we reject Jesus.

SHARE IT

Can you talk to someone today about the dangers of rejecting Jesus?

THE BOTTOM LINE

God is in control, but we are responsible for our actions.

➔ TAKE IT FURTHER

More on God's big plan on page 118.

The missing link

> One of the main ambitions of **engage** is to encourage you to get stuck into God's Word. Each issue, TOOLBOX gives you tips, tools and advice for wrestling with the Bible and understanding it more.

Here are some of the most boring words in the English language: *if, therefore, because, since, but.* Yet (that's another one!) in the Bible, they're vital. They're all linking words. When you see one, take notice and ask: *'What's it doing there?'*

THEREFORE...

Linking words not only help the flow of a Bible passage, they show us how different bits fit together. When you see **'therefore'**, you need to look at what comes immediately before it.

I am sending you out like sheep among wolves. Therefore be as shrewd as snakes and as innocent as doves. (Matthew 10 v 16)

Jesus' instruction to be shrewd but innocent isn't a random piece of advice. The reason comes before the 'therefore' — Jesus was sending them into hostile territory so they needed

to be prepared but stay godly.

'For' works in a similar way:
Therefore, since we have a great high priest who has gone through the heavens, Jesus the Son of God, let us hold firmly to the faith we profess. For we do not have a high priest who is unable to sympathise with our weaknesses, but we have one who has been tempted in every way, just as we are — yet was without sin. (Hebrews 4 v 14–15)

We're told the reason why we should hold firmly to the faith **after** the 'for'.

IF...

'If you're confronted by an angry hippo you should climb the nearest tree and scream for help.' The **'if'** statement tells us that a certain action is required in a certain situation. But if there are no hippos around, you'd look pretty stupid climbing a tree and yelling for help. The advice

is conditional on the circumstances. Here's a Bible example:

The Lord will make you the head, not the tail. If you pay attention to the commands of the Lord your God that I give you this day and carefully follow them, you will always be at the top, never at the bottom ... However, if you do not obey the Lord your God and do not carefully follow all his commands and decrees I am giving you today, all these curses will come upon you and overtake you. (Deuteronomy 28 v 13, 15)

God's blessing is conditional on the Israelites keeping their part of the covenant agreement.

Some *'if'* statements in the Bible aren't conditional and don't suggest uncertainty. Check out **2 Peter 2 v 4–9**. When Peter says *'if'* God did these things, he's not doubting that God did them. Peter uses *'if'* in the same way we use *'because'*. He's saying: 'Look at God's track record' — *if* He's done it before (which He *has*), then He knows what to do this time.

SO THAT...

One final ultra-important linking phrase is **'so that'**. Sometimes it's there to tell us the purpose behind something: *'My dear children, I write this to you so that you will not sin.'* (1 John 2 v 1)

Sometimes it introduces the result of something: *'Meanwhile, when a crowd of many thousands had gathered, so that they were trampling on one another.'* (Luke 12 v 1)

You have to use the context to decide which it is. In this case it's fairly obvious that trampling on people wasn't the purpose of the gathering!

GIVE IT A GO

- Read Titus chapter 2 and list all the linking words you find.
- What's the significance of the *'for'* that links the two halves of the passage? (v11)
- How would the thrust of the passage be seriously altered if verses 11–14 weren't there?
- There are three *so thats* in verses 1–10 What's the repeated reason for Christians to live godly lives?

Words like *if, therefore, but, so that* and *because* may be short and dull, but in the Bible they link important ideas and teaching. They shed light on what a passage is really saying. So look out for them as you continue to dig into God's awesome Word.

Ideas taken from Dig Deeper by Nigel Beynon and Andrew Sach (available from www.thegoodbook.com).

49 Hail to the king

Story so far: God's people, the Israelites, were slaves in Egypt. God chose Moses to lead them out of captivity but Pharaoh refused to let them go. So far, God has sent six plagues on Egypt, but Pharaoh won't budge.

👁 Read Exodus 9 v 13–26

ENGAGE YOUR BRAIN

▶ What was the threat to Pharaoh and Egypt? (v14)

▶ Why didn't God just quickly destroy the Egyptians? (v15–16)

▶ What happened to the people who ignored God's warning? (v21, v25)

▶ Where did it not hail? (v26)

God could have easily wiped out the Egyptians to free the Israelites. But He showed His compassion by continuing to give Pharaoh another chance. The Lord was also using the Egyptians as an example to the whole world. Everyone would see His power and how He rescued His people (v16). Notice that, yet again, the Israelites were unharmed.

👁 Read verses 27–35

▶ What surprising things did Pharaoh say? (v27–28)

▶ But what did Moses know? (v30)

▶ Was he right? (v34–35)

▶ What did God show by stopping the hail storm? (v29)

God hit Egypt with its worse hail storm in history — barley, flax, animals and slaves were destroyed. It was so terrible that Pharaoh admitted he was in the wrong and promised to release God's people. But Moses knew that as soon as the hail stopped, Pharaoh's heart would harden again.

PRAY ABOUT IT

By commanding a huge hail storm, God showed how powerful He is — He's in charge of the whole earth. Bow down before our all-powerful God right now. Praise Him for being in control and thank Him for the amazing world He's created and rules.

THE BOTTOM LINE

God rules the earth.

➡ TAKE IT FURTHER

Feel free to check out page 118.

50 | Day of the locust

Pharaoh remained stubborn, refusing to let the Israelites go worship God in the desert. To bring the Egyptians to their knees again God would now send a plague of... er... locusts? That doesn't sound very scary.

👁 Read Exodus 10 v 1–6

ENGAGE YOUR BRAIN

▶ *Why did God allow Pharaoh's heart to be hardened? (v2)*

▶ *What did Pharaoh refuse to do? (v3)*

▶ *What did God promise as punishment this time?*

Pharaoh refused to let the Israelites worship God and so was rightly punished. And through the way God dealt with the Egyptians, people everywhere would hear of God's power and know that He is the one true God.

Despite all the plagues, Pharaoh refused to admit that God was in charge, and he brought more pain and terror on his people.

👁 Read verses 7–20

▶ *What offer did Pharaoh make? (v11)*

▶ *How did Pharaoh react to the locust infestation? (v16–17)*

▶ *What happened again? (v20)*

Pharaoh's officials begged him to let the Israelites worship God in the desert. But Pharaoh was stubborn and proud and would only let the men go. He still refused to obey God. Then after the locusts had done their damage, Pharaoh admitted his sin. But as soon as the locusts had gone, he refused to release God's people.

THINK IT THROUGH

▶ *Do you ever say sorry to God but not really mean it?*

▶ *Or promise to change your ways but not do it?*

PRAY ABOUT IT

Talk to God honestly about these things. Ask Him to help you truly change your ways for the better.

➔ TAKE IT FURTHER

More stuff on page 119.

51

In the dark

Close your eyes. Keep them shut and try walking to the bathroom.
Not easy, is it? Imagine living in total darkness for three whole days. Pharaoh didn't enjoy it...

👁 Read Exodus 10 v 21–29

ENGAGE YOUR BRAIN

▶ *What deal did Pharaoh offer this time? (v24)*

▶ *But how did Moses respond? (v25–26)*

▶ *What was the predictable outcome? (v27–29)*

The Egyptians were terrified about being thrown into total darkness for three days. But Pharaoh still refused to bow down to God. He still wanted things *his* way. He soon learned that you can't bargain with God.

Moses rightly stood up to Pharaoh and didn't give in to his demands. He insisted on obeying all of God's commands and not just part of them. Moses actually commanded the king of Egypt, telling him what to do! (v25) He knew that God was much more powerful than Pharaoh.

THINK IT THROUGH

▶ *Do you ever compromise with your faith?*

▶ *What wrong things do you refuse to cut out of your life?*

▶ *When do you give God half measures rather than full obedience?*

PRAY ABOUT IT

Talk openly with God. Ask Him to help you not compromise when it comes to obeying Him. Thank Him that He's more powerful than anything or anyone and can help you in huge ways.

THE BOTTOM LINE

Don't compromise when it comes to obeying God.

➡ TAKE IT FURTHER

No *Take it Further* today, sorry.

52 | Final warning

Pharaoh and the Egyptians have had nine warnings from God already. God would give them one more chance to let His people go before hitting them with the most devastating plague of all.

👁 Read Exodus 11 v 1–8

ENGAGE YOUR BRAIN

▶ What did God say would happen? (v1)

▶ What else had God done for His people? (v3)

▶ What was the very bad news for the Egyptians? (v5–6)

▶ How would things be different for the Israelites? (v7–8)

Why would God do such a horrific thing as that? It was punishment for Pharaoh and the Egyptians for enslaving God's people, treating them cruelly (remember Pharaoh slaughtering baby Israelite boys?) and refusing to let them go.

It would show Pharaoh once and for all that God was in charge, not him. And only something as awful as this final plague would make Pharaoh finally let God's people go.

👁 Read verses 9–10

▶ How does v10 sum up chapters 7–11 of Exodus?

Pharaoh refused to change. He refused to obey God and brought disaster on his people. *'The Lord hardened Pharaoh's heart'* doesn't mean Pharaoh had no choice in the matter. He had already **chosen** to reject God (Exodus 8 v 15). So God made Pharaoh what he had chosen to be. Pharaoh got the punishment he deserved.

PRAY ABOUT IT

Pray for people you know who refuse to live God's way. Ask the Lord to soften their hearts so that they turn to Him, and live for Him, not themselves.

➔ TAKE IT FURTHER

Promises promises on page 119.

53 | Making a meal of it

It's getting to the crunch point in Egypt. God would send a final plague, killing the eldest son in each Egyptian family. But what about Israelite families? And what have lambs got to do with it?

👁 **Read Exodus 12 v 1–11**

ENGAGE YOUR BRAIN

▷ *In your own words, describe what the Israelites had to do.*

▷ *Why did they have to eat in a hurry, with their walking clothes on? (v11)*

God gave His people specific instructions for the **Passover**. They had to do these things to be rescued by God. And they had to be ready for Him to rescue them.

👁 **Read verses 12–13**

▷ *What would God do to Egypt?*

▷ *How would the lambs' blood save the Israelites?*

The lamb was killed instead of the firstborn son in each Israelite family. The blood of the lamb was protection. If there was lamb's blood on the door frame, the Lord would pass over that house. The eldest son could say: *'That lamb died in my place'.*

The lamb's death is a picture of what Jesus would do 1500 years later. He would die on the cross to take the punishment we deserve for our sins against God. Christians can look to Jesus and say: *'He died in my place'.*

SHARE IT

Who can you explain the whole Passover thing to? How can you link it to what Jesus has done for you?

PRAY ABOUT IT

If you're a Christian, thank God for sending Jesus to die in your place. Praise Him that on the day of judgment, He will pass over you and not punish you, because of Jesus' death.

→ TAKE IT FURTHER

More on the lamb and Jesus on p119.

54 Feast first

It's the night of God's final plague on Egypt.
Time to eat some strange bread and tasty lamb.
One of the most important meals ever.

👁 Read Exodus 12 v 14–20

ENGAGE YOUR BRAIN

▶ What did the Israelites have to do? (v15–16)

▶ Why? (v17)

▶ What would happen to anyone who disobeyed God? (v19)

God was about to rescue them from slavery in Egypt — it would be a day to remember forever. They would commemorate it by having a special feast week, by not eating food with yeast in it, and by resting from work. Celebrating the feast every year would remind the Israelites of God's great rescue.

Anyone who disobeyed God's command would be **cut off** from His people. That's how seriously God treats sin. Anyone who refuses to obey Him will be **cut off** from Him forever.

👁 Read verses 21–28

▶ Why did they have to put blood on their door frames and stay indoors? (v23)

The lamb's blood would save them from God's punishment. And that goes for us too. We've all disobeyed God and all deserve to be cut off from Him. But God sent Jesus to rescue people. Jesus, the Lamb of God, died so those who trust His blood (death) to rescue them will not be punished by God. Incredible.

PRAY ABOUT IT

You're on your own today.
▶ What do you want to say to God?
▶ What do you need to say to Him?

THE BOTTOM LINE

Remember God rescuing His people.

➡ TAKE IT FURTHER

More about yeast and feasts on p119.

55

Time to go

It's the big one — the tenth and final plague. The Israelites have eaten their lamb, put the blood on their door-posts, got their yeastless dough and are ready to leave...

Read Exodus 12 v 29–32

ENGAGE YOUR BRAIN

▷ How did Pharaoh and the Egyptians react to this final plague? (v30)

▷ What did Pharaoh do, at last?

Pharaoh had repeatedly refused to obey God and release the Israelites. God kept His promise and the eldest son in each Egyptian family died. Only after this final horrific plague did Pharaoh finally obey God and let the Israelites go.

Read verses 33–42

▷ What did the Egyptian people do? (v33, v36)

▷ How were the Israelites able to escape Egypt? (v37)

▷ How did they remember it for years to come? (v42)

The Egyptians were so terrified of God, they *wanted* the Israelites to leave! They even gave them gold and silver, as God had said they would (Exodus 3 v 21–22).

Feel the relief — centuries of slavery in a foreign land, then God's dramatic rescue during a midnight slaughter. The New Testament tells us this rescue is a picture of a far greater one, when Jesus died on the cross to rescue His people from slavery to sin.

PRAY ABOUT IT

Read through this story again, thanking God for this amazing rescue. Then reflect on Jesus' death on the cross. Praise God for this ultimate rescue.

THE BOTTOM LINE

God rescues His people.

→ TAKE IT FURTHER

Feeling sleepy? Try page 119.

56 God's people

'ALL ABSEILERS MUST WEAR A HELMET'
To do certain things, you have to follow important rules. LIke wearing a helmet before throwing yourself off a cliff face. No helmet? No abseiling.

The Israelites had to obey special rules to take part in the Passover feast.

◉ Read Exodus 12 v 43–51

ENGAGE YOUR BRAIN

▶ Who couldn't eat the Passover meal? (v43, v45, v48)

▶ What did you have to do to qualify? (v44, v48)

Every male wanting to take part had to be an Israelite, one of God's people. The mark of this was being circumcised — having part of the skin around the penis cut off. Ouch. It was a sign that a man or boy belonged to God's people.

Since Jesus died on the cross for us, we don't have to be circumcised to show that we are part of God's family. So what do you need to become one of God's people, a Christian?

◉ Read John 3 v 3

When you believe that Jesus died for you, God forgives your sin and changes you. It's like being born again. You start living for God instead of yourself.

SHARE IT

If someone asked you: 'How do you become a Christian?' how would you answer them? Plan out your response on paper.

PRAY ABOUT IT

Are you part of God's people? If so, get praising God. If not, what are you going to do about it?

→ TAKE IT FURTHER

More on circumcision on page 119.

57 | Remember remember

How do you remember stuff, like facts for exams?
Do you write them out loads of times, or maybe make
up bizarre songs to help you remember. Check out the
Israelites' weird way of remembering God's rescue.

Read Exodus 13 v 1–10

ENGAGE YOUR BRAIN

▶ How did the Israelites celebrate
the day God rescued them from
Egypt? (v6–7)

▶ What would it remind them of?
(v8–9)

▶ What did God promise His
people? (v5)

For centuries, God had promised to
give His people their own land —
Canaan. When they eventually arrived
there, they were to hold this feast
and remember God rescuing them.
It would also remind them of God's
awesome power and their need to
live His way — keeping His law on
their lips.

Read verses 11–16

▶ Why did they dedicate all their
firstborn to God? (v14–16)

Dedicating each firstborn child to
God reminded the Israelites that they
were God's *'firstborn'* — His chosen
people, rescued by Him.

Christians have been rescued by God
from the punishment they deserve
for their sin. We were all ruled by the
sin in our lives, but Jesus died on the
cross to pay the price and buy us back
(*redeem* us).

PRAY ABOUT IT

Thank God for His amazing rescue.
Ask Him to help you take His Word
— in the Bible — to heart, so that
His law is on your lips and you live
to please Him.

→ TAKE IT FURTHER

Remember to go to page 120.

58

God's guidance

The Israelites are on the run from Egypt and they're not safe yet. The Egyptian army is behind them and the Philistine army is in front of them. Will they fight or run?

👁 Read Exodus 13 v 17–22

ENGAGE YOUR BRAIN

▶ *Why did God lead His people away from the Philistines? (v17)*

▶ *How did God lead them? (v21)*

God knew the Israelites would freak out and give up if they faced the mighty Philistine army. So He took them the long way round, leading them in a spectacular way — in a pillar of cloud by day and a pillar of fire at night. He didn't leave His people for one second; He was guiding them all the way (v22).

👁 Read verse 19

▶ *Why was Moses carrying Joseph's bones around with Him???*

Talk about having a skeleton in your closet! Remember Joseph from the last issue of *engage*? God had promised Joseph's family that He would give them the country of Canaan to live in. Even though Joseph

lived and died in Egypt, he trusted God's promise to take the Israelites to Canaan. He showed his great faith in God by asking for his bones to be carried to Canaan and buried there (Genesis 50 v 24–26).

GET ON WITH IT

▶ *Are you letting God lead you through life?*

▶ *How can you follow Him more?*

▶ *Which of God's promises in the Bible can you hold on to?*

PRAY ABOUT IT

Thank God that He guides His people through life and never leaves them. And thank God that He always keeps His promises.

THE BOTTOM LINE

God sticks with His people.

➡ TAKE IT FURTHER

More on Joe's bones on page 120.

71

59 | In a tight spot

How do you react when you're in a tight spot?
Curl up into a ball? Come out fighting? Blame
God? Trust Him to get you through?

Read Exodus 14 v 1–9

ENGAGE YOUR BRAIN

▶ *What was God's plan? (v1–4)*

▶ *What would it achieve? (v4)*

▶ *What did Pharaoh and the Egyptians do?*

It seemed like a weird plan that would trap the Israelites — turning around and heading back towards Egypt. Crazy. But God was in complete control. He would rescue His people. He would punish the evil Egyptians. And everyone would know that He was the Lord (v4)!

Read verses 10–14

▶ *What ridiculous claims did the Israelites make? (v11–12)*

▶ *How much were they trusting God?*

▶ *What was Moses' brilliant, inspiring answer?*

The Israelites were so terrified of the Egyptian army they lost all faith in God to protect them. But Moses knew God was in control and would keep His promise to crush the Egyptians and rescue His people. He knew that it wasn't down to their strength — it was all down to God (v14). They just had to sit still; God would fight for them.

PRAY ABOUT IT

Say sorry to God for specific times you've doubted Him. Ask Him to help you trust Him more.

THE BOTTOM LINE

Trust in the Lord.

→ TAKE IT FURTHER

A little more on page 120.

60 Walking through water

The Israelites were terrified. The huge Egyptian army was hot on their heels and they seemed to be trapped against the banks of the Red Sea. Many of them doubted that God would really rescue them.

👁 Read Exodus 14 v 15–22

ENGAGE YOUR BRAIN

▶ *What did God say He would do? (v16–17)*

▶ *Why? (v18)*

▶ *What else did He do for His people? (v20)*

God promised to rescue His people and keep His word. He put the pillar of cloud between them and the Egyptians, plunging the Egyptians into darkness. He then parted the Red Sea so the Israelites could walk through on dry ground. Amazing.

God wants everyone to know that He is in control of everything. To know that He is the only God and worship Him.

👁 Read verses 23–31

▶ *How did God punish Pharaoh and the Egyptians for sinning against Him?*

▶ *What happened to God's people and how did they respond? (v31)*

▶ *How has their attitude changed since v10–12?*

God's enemies got the punishment they deserved. Ultimately, God will punish everyone who refuses to obey Him. And He will rescue His people. When the Israelites saw what He had done, they feared God and put their trust in Him. Finally.

PRAY ABOUT IT

Does this incredible rescue inspire you to trust God and shout thanks to Him? As you praise God for this fantastic rescue mission, thank Him for the ultimate rescue — achieved by Jesus on the cross.

THE BOTTOM LINE

God rescues His people and punishes His enemies.

→ TAKE IT FURTHER

Terrifying truth on page 120.

61 | Sing when you're winning

Is there anything that always gets you singing? Maybe you can't resist a bit of karaoke. Or joining in with your team's chants. Moses and the Israelites couldn't stop themselves from singing to God...

👁 **Read Exodus 15 v 1–2**

ENGAGE YOUR BRAIN

▶ What were they excitedly singing about God?

▶ Which lines can you echo?

God had rescued His people from slavery and defeated their enemies in spectacular style. And now they wanted to sing about it and praise Him. The great thing is that all Christians can sing and shout verse 2. God has saved them from sin. He is their source of strength. He's the one they want to sing and shout about.

▶ Is this true for you?

👁 **Read verses 3–12**

▶ How many different phrases do they use to describe God defeating the Egyptians?

▶ What do they conclude about God? (v12)

They had seen God's awesome power right in front of their eyes. He destroyed the massive, terrifying Egyptian army easily. No one can go against God and win. No one is more majestic, more holy, more awesome, more glorious, more wonderful than the Lord.

SHARE IT

How can you 'sing' about God — tell others how incredible and powerful He is?

PRAY ABOUT IT

Put verses 2 and 12 into your own words as you praise our amazing God right now.

THE BOTTOM LINE

The Lord is my strength, my salvation.

→ TAKE IT FURTHER

More singing on page 120.

62 Raise the praise

God has rescued His people from slavery. He has brought them out of Egypt and drowned the Egyptian army. Moses and the Israelites can't stop singing and worshipping their awesome God.

Read Exodus 15 v 13–18

ENGAGE YOUR BRAIN

▶ What did the future hold for God's people? (v13, v17)

▶ What will happen to their enemies? (v14–16)

▶ What did they recognise about God? (v18)

Suddenly, the future looked much brighter for the Israelites. There were many enemies ahead of them, but God had already done the hard part — of course He'd protect them against other nations. And give them the land He'd promised (v17). Because of His love for His people, God would lead them and even live with them (v13).

Read verses 19–21

▶ Who else joined in with the singing and dancing?

Everyone was overjoyed that God was with them, leading them. Christians can be just as confident in God as Moses and Miriam were. God has already done so much for them — rescuing them from sin and judgment. They know that no enemy is more powerful than God, and one day He will take them to live with Him forever. The Lord will reign forever!

PRAY ABOUT IT

Read slowly through the verses again, taking time to praise and thank God for all He's done. Nothing can defeat Him. He's the eternal King who rules forever.

THE BOTTOM LINE

God will reign forever!

TAKE IT FURTHER

More on page 121.

63

Three days later...

God had led His people through the Red Sea and destroyed the Egyptian army. The Israelites were thrilled — praising God and trusting Him to lead them. But would it last?

👁 Read Exodus 15 v 22–24

ENGAGE YOUR BRAIN
▶ *How did the people react to the first bad situation they found themselves in?*

They were in the desert with no clean water to drink, so it's not surprising they grumbled. But they had already forgotten that God had done amazing things for them and He was with them all the way.

We can sometimes be very quick to forget God and all that He's done for us, and start complaining. God had a good reason for not giving them fresh water straightaway. He was testing the Israelites to see if they still trusted Him.

👁 Read verses 25–27
▶ *What did God do? (v25)*

▶ *What did God require of His people? (v26)*

Despite their grumbling, God made the stagnant water sweet and drinkable. And He made His point: *'You've seen all that I've done for you, so trust me and obey me.'* Next issue, we'll discover whether or not they did.

PRAY ABOUT IT
God says the same to us: *'Remember all I've done for you; trust me through the tough times; obey my commands and live my way.'* Ask the Lord to help you do these things.

THE BOTTOM LINE
Trust and obey.

→ TAKE IT FURTHER
Time to dive into the Bible's longest chapter — go to page 121.

64 | Notice the notice

Crucifixion was a horrific punishment, but John doesn't spend any time on the gory details. More important than what happened is WHY it happened.

👁 Read John 19 v 17–22

ENGAGE YOUR BRAIN

🔘 *What facts does John give us about Jesus' execution?*

🔘 *What did Pilate's notice say?*

🔘 *What do you think he meant by it?*

🔘 *What did the chief priests object to about it?*

🔘 *What is so ironic about the notice?*

Yet again in John's Gospel we see people speaking the truth when they weren't intending to. Pilate may have meant the sign sarcastically or to annoy the Jews, but it was the absolute truth. Jesus was the king of the Jews; in fact He is the King of the whole world.

Notice that the sign was written in all the most important languages of Jesus' day — Jesus' death is important for the whole world. EVERYONE needs to know about Jesus' death and understand why He died.

SHARE IT

The truth about Jesus' death is a message for the whole world. That includes the people you know.

🔘 *Who will you tell about Jesus this week?*
🔘 *How will you do it?*

PRAY ABOUT IT

Take some time to think about the amazing truth that the King of everything died on the cross for you, and talk to God about it. You could use Philippians 2 v 5–11 to help you thank God for what Jesus did.

THE BOTTOM LINE

Jesus is the King of everything.

→ TAKE IT FURTHER

More on page 121.

65 All part of the plan

Even the most horrible bits of Jesus' death were part of God's plan. In fact, they were predicted hundreds of years before Jesus was born. Time for some detective work.

Read John 19 v 23–24

ENGAGE YOUR BRAIN
Verse 24 has a quote from Psalm 22. Spend some time reading that psalm now and jot down all the similarities you can find with John's version of Jesus' crucifixion:

For more Old Testament prophecies about Jesus' death, check out the *Take it further* section on page 121.

Read John 19 v 25–27
Even as He is dying, Jesus still shows compassion to other people.

> How does He provide for His mother and His friend?

PRAY ABOUT IT
Look back at all the things you listed on the left. Add the words 'for me' after each one and tell God what that means to you.

THE BOTTOM LINE
Everything Jesus did was part of God's plan.

→ TAKE IT FURTHER
More amazing predictions on page 121.

SHARE IT
Do your friends realise that Jesus' death wasn't just an accident or a miscarriage of justice? Can you show them how accurate the prophecies about Him in the Old Testament are?

66 Finished

It's nearly over. But even as He is dying, Jesus is still doing His Father's work. His death isn't a failure but achieves exactly what He set out to do. This is no defeat: it is the ultimate victory!

👁 Read John 19 v 28–30

ENGAGE YOUR BRAIN

🔹 *According to v28, why does Jesus say He is thirsty?*

🔹 *What do you think the first part of v28 means? What is completed? What is finished? (v30)*

'It is finished' — everything Jesus had come to do was completed. The innocent had died instead of the guilty. The Son had given Himself to set prisoners free. The ransom was paid in full. Jesus died so that sinful people like us could be forgiven.

PRAY ABOUT IT

When you look at the things you've done wrong in your life and feel bad about them, remember that Jesus dealt with sin once and for all on the cross. If you trust in His death in your place, **it is finished**. He has dealt with all your sins — He's taken the punishment you deserve.

Spend some time thanking Him for that right now.

🔹 *How does John describe Jesus' death? (v30)*

🔹 *How is his choice of words unusual?*

Jesus chose when to die — He gave up His own spirit, it was His decision. Look back at how He saw His own death in John 10 v 14–18.

🔹 *How does John 10 v 14–18 help us to understand the events of chapter 19?*

🔹 *What does it tell us about Jesus?*

THE BOTTOM LINE

It is finished. Once and for all.

➔ TAKE IT FURTHER

Turn to page 121 for a song.

67 | Dead certain

Imagine a friend challenging you: 'I don't believe Jesus really died — He just fainted on the cross. He wasn't actually dead.' What would you say to them?

👁 **Read John 19 v 31–37**

ENGAGE YOUR BRAIN

▶ *Why didn't the Jews want the bodies left on the crosses?*

▶ *Why would breaking the victims' legs speed things along a bit?*

▶ *Why didn't they need to break Jesus' legs?*

▶ *What did they do instead?*

Breaking a victim's legs speeded up death because he could no longer lift himself up to breathe properly. The blood and water probably meant they had pierced Jesus' heart — the water coming from the sac surrounding the heart. Proof that He was dead.

SHARE IT

Various people, including some Muslims, don't believe that Jesus actually died on the cross. They think He just fainted and so the resurrection was a big hoax. The Bible is very clear

that Jesus died. The Roman soldiers were expert executioners. The events you've just read about show Jesus was definitely dead. How many critically wounded people do you know who could survive three days in a tomb with no food or water before pushing a huge stone away and claiming to be alive? Get to grips with the facts of the resurrection and share them with those who don't believe.

▶ *What was the real reason behind the way the soldiers behaved (v36–37)?*
▶ *How do we know this is what happened (v35)?*
▶ *Why has John bothered to write any of this down (v35)?*

GET ON WITH IT

Have you believed? This isn't just an interesting piece of history. It's life-changing stuff.

➡ TAKE IT FURTHER

More prophecies on page 121. More resurrection evidence on page 90.

68 Dead and buried?

Despite the grief that Jesus' followers are feeling at this time, things are not hopeless. As Jesus' body is prepared for burial, we get the feeling that there's something more to come.

👁 Read John 19 v 38–42

ENGAGE YOUR BRAIN

ⓘ *What do we know about Joseph and Nicodemus? Jot it down.*

Despite being intimidated by the Jewish authorities, Joseph and Nicodemus were determined to give Jesus a decent burial – new tomb and expensive spices to embalm the body.

ⓘ *Why is it important to know that they had to get Pilate's permission to remove the body?*

ⓘ *How does this support the fact the Jesus was definitely dead?*

ⓘ *Why is it important that the tomb is new and empty (no other bodies already in it — v41) for what happens in chapter 20?*

Look back at John 3 v 1–15 and 7 v 50–51. Think about how much Nicodemus has changed.

PRAY ABOUT IT

Jesus changes people. God can turn His enemies into His friends; in fact that's what Jesus died to accomplish. Ask Him now to do that for people you know who are currently His enemies.

THE BOTTOM LINE

The tomb is not the end of the story.

→ TAKE IT FURTHER

More about Jesus' resurrection on page 121.

69 ┆ Rise and shine ┆

Remember that John is writing about events he experienced first hand. See how many eye-witness details you can spot as you read today's passage.

◉ Read John 20 v 1–9

ENGAGE YOUR BRAIN

▶ What does Mary think has happened? (v2)

▶ But what did Peter see? (v6-7)

▶ Does that sound like the work of grave robbers?

The burial clothes were left behind and folded neatly — clearly not the work of grab-and-run grave robbers. Unlikely that anyone else would have gone to the trouble of removing them either. No, it's as if Jesus just stepped out of them or passed through them.

▶ What did John realise (v8)?

▶ What had he forgotten (v9)?

▶ What should our response to these events be (look ahead to v29)?

Yet again, everything Jesus did fulfilled what had been written about Him centuries before. This was all part of God's amazing plan.

TALK IT OVER

Get together with other Christians and talk about why it matters that Jesus didn't just die for our sins but that He rose again as well. This is vital stuff — that's why John gives us the details and evidence.

THE BOTTOM LINE

The tomb was empty.

➔ TAKE IT FURTHER

What did Jesus' resurrection achieve? Find out on page 122.

70 | He's alive!

The mystery of the empty tomb is about to be solved. Mary comes face to face with the risen Lord Jesus — it's an incredible moment.

👁 Read John 20 v 10–16

ENGAGE YOUR BRAIN

▶ What question is Mary asked? (v13, v15)

▶ What's her response?

▶ How does Jesus treat her?

Mary wasn't just sniffling, the word for crying here means *'wailing'* — serious grief. But Jesus speaks to her by name and gives her the best comfort of all —— He is alive! Imagine her pure, ecstatic joy.

▶ How does Mary respond?

👁 Read verses 17–18

Jesus will soon be returning to His Father — look at how He describes the relationship that we can also have with God in v17. In the meantime, there's work to be done.

▶ What job does Jesus give Mary?

GET ON WITH IT

Mary can't keep this amazing news to herself. She obeys Jesus and tells His followers what she has seen.

▶ Can you share the good news that Jesus is alive with someone today or tomorrow?

THE BOTTOM LINE

Jesus is alive!

➔ TAKE IT FURTHER

Get reflective on page 122.

71 ┊ Forgiven followers

Later on that first amazing Easter Sunday, Jesus appeared to His disciples. Yes, the same few who had deserted Him when He was arrested and were terrified that the Jews might go after them next.

👁 Read John 20 v 19–23

ENGAGE YOUR BRAIN

▶ *How would you sum up the state of the disciples in v19?*

▶ *How does Jesus greet them? Why might He have chosen those words?*

▶ *How does He prove that He isn't a ghost and they're not hallucinating?*

▶ *What job does Jesus give the disciples? (v21)*

▶ *How does He equip them?*

Jesus appoints His followers to carry on the job of sharing the good news of God's offer of free forgiveness. Once He returns to His Father, He will send His Spirit to help them in this awesome task. Verse 23 doesn't mean that the disciples can forgive people on their own, but rather that in sharing the good news about Jesus, people will accept it and be forgiven or, sadly, reject it and remain unforgiven.

PRAY ABOUT IT

Thank God for the people who shared the good news about Jesus with you. Ask for His help to pass it on to others.

THE BOTTOM LINE

Forgiveness is found in Jesus.

→ TAKE IT FURTHER

See lives transformed on page 122.

72 | Trust Thomas |

Thomas (or 'doubting Thomas' as the poor guy has been known for centuries) gets a bit of a bad press. But would you have behaved any differently in the circumstances?

👁 Read John 20 v 24–29

ENGAGE YOUR BRAIN

▶ What wouldn't Thomas believe? (v24-25)

▶ How does Jesus get rid of Thomas' doubts? (v27)

▶ What is Thomas' response? Who does he say Jesus is?

This isn't just a response of 'Wow!' Now that he knows that Jesus has risen from the dead, Thomas realises that Jesus must be God and worships Him the way he should.

▶ What else does Jesus say to Thomas? (v29)

Let's face it, Thomas' reluctance to believe such an incredible thing seems perfectly reasonable, but look at what he was saying. 'These 10 guys who I've known for at least 3 years and know are reliable, tell me about something they all have witnessed

and swear is the truth, but I'm not going to believe them.' Jesus points out that the other disciples' eye-witness evidence was enough to go on. Enough for Thomas and enough for us (v29).

GET ON WITH IT

We haven't seen the risen Jesus in the flesh, but we have heard the reliable evidence of His disciples.
▶ Have you accepted it?
▶ Do you believe?
▶ Is Jesus your Lord and your God?

PRAY ABOUT IT

Jesus is gracious to Thomas and gives him what he needs to believe. Thank God that He relates to us as individuals and understands all our weaknesses.

THE BOTTOM LINE

We have enough evidence to believe.

→ TAKE IT FURTHER

More more more on page 122.

73 | Reason for writing

Have you ever flicked ahead to the end of a book to see what happens? As we near the end of John's gospel, John tells us why he bothered to write it in the first place.

👁 Read John 20 v 30–31

ENGAGE YOUR BRAIN

▶ *Look at verse 30 – what did Jesus do and who saw what He did?*

▶ *Jesus did lots of 'signs' — things that pointed to His identity. Can you remember some from earlier in John's Gospel and what they showed about Jesus? Jot them down below:*

Once again John reminds us in v30 that he is writing an eye-witness account. Like Thomas we should and can trust John's testimony because he was there, he saw it all happen.

▶ *What does John say about what his Gospel does and doesn't cover?*

There are so many other things John could have written about that Jesus did — you can find some of them in the other Gospel accounts. But check this out: *'If every one of them were written down, I suppose that even the whole world would not have room for the books that would be written.'* (John 21 v 25)

▶ *So what was John's purpose in writing what he did? (v31)*

▶ *Why is it so important that people believe this?*

PRAY ABOUT IT

Life or death. That's what's at stake here. Believe in Jesus and have life in His name or reject Him and perish (remember John 3 v 16–18?). Pray for people you know who haven't yet believed in Jesus.

THE BOTTOM LINE

Choose life.

→ TAKE IT FURTHER

A tiny bit more on page 122.

74 What a catch!

Jesus appears to His disciples for the third time after His resurrection. This time He even cooks them breakfast!

👁 Read John 21 v 1–6

ENGAGE YOUR BRAIN

▶ *Who was part of the fishing party?*

▶ *Did they have much luck before they saw Jesus?*

▶ *How about after?*

▶ *What does this show us about Jesus?*

It's not explained why the disciples don't recognise Jesus at first (compare Mary in chapter 20). But once He acts — gives them another sign — they know exactly who He is. As the kids' song puts it: *'only God could do that!'*

▶ *Read Luke 5 v 1–11. Why might the sign in John 21 have seemed familiar?*

👁 Read John 21 v 7–14

▶ *How does Peter respond when he realises it's Jesus?*

▶ *How does Jesus show His care for His friends? (v12)*

▶ *Can you spot more details which show that this is an eye-witness account?*

PRAY ABOUT IT

Thank God for the care Jesus shows for His followers — even down to cooking them breakfast! Thank Him for specific ways He's shown His care for you.

THE BOTTOM LINE

Jesus cares for you.

→ TAKE IT FURTHER

Chase away your worries on page 122.

75 | Peter pardoned

Remember the miserable events of chapter 18? Peter denied he even knew Jesus three times. Now that they finally get some one-to-one time, how will Jesus react?

👁 **Read John 21 v 15–17**

ENGAGE YOUR BRAIN

▶ *Why do you think Jesus asks the question in verse 15? (Clue: look back to 13 v 37 and Mark 14 v 29.)*

▶ *Does Peter react with the same pride he showed before?*

▶ *What's his reply?*

▶ *What did Jesus tell him to do?*

Sheep were a common picture of God's people. By asking Peter to feed and take care of His sheep, Jesus is giving him the job of looking after and caring for His disciples.

▶ *Why do you think Jesus asks him the same question three times?*

Jesus graciously gives Peter the opportunity to cancel out his three-time denial by letting him affirm his love for Jesus three times. Beautiful.

PRAY ABOUT IT

Thank God that He understands our weaknesses and helps us to start again.

Read 2 Corinthians 5 v 17. Spend some time thanking God for wiping out the past and for giving you a new start.

THE BOTTOM LINE

Our God offers a fresh start.

➡ **TAKE IT FURTHER**

Wise words from Peter on page 122.

76

Follow me

We've established that following Jesus is the smart move — but what will it involve? Let's listen in to a conversation between Jesus and some of His first followers to find out.

Read John 21 v 18–25

ENGAGE YOUR BRAIN

▶ What warning does Jesus give Peter about what it will mean to follow Him (v18)?

▶ What does He still command Peter to do (v19)?

Following Jesus means giving up everything. In Luke 9 v 23–34 Jesus says: *'If anyone would come after me, he must deny himself and take up his cross daily and follow me. For whoever wants to save his life will lose it, but whoever loses his life for me will save it.'*

It's a big decision to follow Jesus. In some countries it could cost you your life. But eternal life is much more valuable. As the martyred missionary Jim Elliot said: *'He is no fool who gives what he cannot keep to gain what he cannot lose'.*

▶ What does Peter get distracted by (v21)?

▶ What is Jesus' response (v22)?

It's so easy to compare ourselves to other Christians. What are they doing? How come they get away with that? Why can't I be in their situation? Jesus says: 'Forget about anyone else. You need to follow me.'

PRAY ABOUT IT

Ask for God's help to keep your eyes fixed on Jesus, to live for Him without getting distracted by anyone else.

▶ How does John remind us that we can trust what he has written (v24)?

THE BOTTOM LINE

Following Jesus costs everything but the rewards are priceless.

➡ TAKE IT FURTHER

The last word on John's Gospel is on page 123.

Did the resurrection really happen?

Each issue in TRICKY, we tackle those mind-bendingly difficult questions that confuse us all, as well as questions that friends bombard us with to catch us out.
This time: **Did Jesus really come back from the dead?**

Elvis is alive! Spotted behind the counter of a local burger bar. Are the claims that Jesus rose from the dead just another dubious conspiracy theory?

Well, the apostle Paul said: *'If Christ has not been raised, your faith is futile; you are still in your sins'* (1 Corinthians 15 v 17); which makes it a massively important question to answer. Christianity stand or falls on the resurrection of Jesus Christ. So let's see if it really holds together by looking at the arguments against it.

fainted, is it likely that after three days in a cold tomb with no food, water or medical attention that He could have pushed a huge stone away and then convinced people that He had conquered death?

OK, so maybe someone did die on that cross, but it wasn't Jesus. The suggestion of mistaken identity is not very plausible either. After all, everyone in Jerusalem was talking about Jesus — could Judas, the Jewish leaders, Herod, and Pilate the Roman governor all have been mistaken? No chance.

EXPLANATION 1
JESUS DIDN'T REALLY DIE
Some people, especially some Muslims, argue that Jesus fainted on the cross and was mistakenly assumed to be dead. But let's not forget that the Romans were expert executioners. If you read John 19 v 28–34, you'll notice that not only did the Roman soldiers pronounce Jesus dead, but they stuck a spear into His side just to be sure. And even if Jesus had just

EXPLANATION 2
JESUS DIDN'T REALLY RISE
So perhaps Jesus did die but He wasn't raised back to life — His body must have been stolen by grave robbers. But the tomb was under armed guard (Matthew 27 v 62–66) and the penalty for a soldier deserting his post was death! Besides, why would robbers have left the expensive grave clothes? It would be a lot of time and trouble to remove them in

the middle of a secret body theft. Maybe the body was stolen by Jesus' disciples? Is it likely that a bunch of terrified men (Mark 14 v 50) would have mounted a surprise attack on the Roman guards to steal the body? Later on, many of the disciples were killed for their faith — if they knew that the resurrection was a hoax, surely they would have admitted that to save their lives?

Perhaps the body was stolen by the Jewish leaders or Roman authorities? Jesus' enemies would have produced the corpse if they had it, to disprove what the disciples were claiming about Jesus' resurrection?

Well, what if the body spontaneously combusted — just exploded and nothing was left — hence the empty tomb? Well, spontaneous combustion is a debated phenomenon to begin with, but even supposed cases have left body parts behind. And why would the grave clothes not have burned up (John 20 v 5–8)?

The disciples must have got the wrong tomb then. But it wasn't just the women who found the tomb empty — Peter and John double checked (Luke 23 v 50 – 24 v 12). Surely if a mistake had been made, someone would have pointed it out?

Obviously the disciples hallucinated the whole thing. They just thought they had seen Jesus alive again.

Go and read 1 Corinthians 15 v 3–8. These facts don't fit with medical reports about hallucinations. And you're still left with the problem of what happened to the body.

OK, OK, maybe the disciples were simply lying about the whole thing. But surely someone would have cracked? Plus, would you really be prepared to die for something you knew was a lie?

SO WHAT?

We've seen that the evidence for the resurrection is far stronger than any reasons people give for doubting it, so we need to ask ourselves this question: if Jesus really did rise from the dead, what does it mean for me?

Well, it's a lot more significant than Elvis being found behind the tills at Burger Bonanza. It's life-changing. It means Jesus is exactly who He claims to be — the Son of God with the power to forgive your sins and give you eternal life.

Ecclesiastes

Everything's meaningless

'Meaningless! Meaningless!' says the Teacher. 'Utterly meaningless! Everything is meaningless!' (Ecclesiastes 1 v 2)

Not the most encouraging start to a book you've ever read, is it? So can we expect to make any sense of this book at all? Well, bizarrely, the best place to start is Genesis chapter 3. Remember the whole fruit episode, or what theologians call 'the Fall'? Take a minute now to remind yourself — go and read it.

So, Adam and Eve disobey God, rebel against His rule and things turn pear-shaped (sorry!). Work becomes a burden, relationships are full of conflict and death enters the world. And that's the world we're living in now and the world the Teacher in Ecclesiastes was writing about. It's a long way from the perfect world God created; instead it's characterised by injustice, sorrow, and huge frustration.

So the word *'meaningless'* (which appears repeatedly in Ecclesiastes) could be better translated 'fallen'. But the Teacher couldn't see the whole picture. He has glimpses of hope — that God will judge evil somehow — but he doesn't know about Jesus.

We live after Jesus' death and resurrection and we know that God hasn't left things in a frustrating mess. God's ultimate plan for His people and His creation is to experience freedom and life through His Son, Jesus.

So when you read Ecclesiastes, remember that the Teacher (probably King Solomon) was writing about the world we're in now, but also remember that in Christ there is an answer to the meaninglessness and frustration we see around us.

77 | Same old, same old

For the writer of Ecclesiastes, life is like a broken pencil... pointless (groan). But why does he think that? Is life really meaningless? Will this book give us any answers or will it just make us depressed?

👁 Read Ecclesiastes 1 v 1–11

ENGAGE YOUR BRAIN

▷ What's the Teacher's big conclusion? (v2)

▷ Do you agree with him?

▷ Why/why not?

As the Teacher looks at the world — everything 'under the sun' (keep your eyes open for this expression as it comes up a lot), he sees the same old thing happening again and again.

▷ What examples from nature does he use to prove his point? (v3–7)

▷ What examples from human life does he use? (v3–4, v8–11)

Is there really nothing new under the sun (v9)? What about inventions? The Teacher seems to be talking more about history repeating itself, people making the same mistakes time after time. So is he right? Is life pointless?

Does anything give it meaning? Well, read Ecclesiastes to the end and you might get some answers, but at the moment things look pretty bleak.

SHARE IT

Do you or your friends ever feel like this? Chat to them; do they think life has a meaning and purpose? What is it? Can you share what your meaning and purpose of life is?

THE BOTTOM LINE

There's nothing new under the sun.

➔ TAKE IT FURTHER

Learn something new on page 123.

78 | Trivial pursuit

'The truth is out there.' So the Teacher sets out to try and discover if there is any meaning in life or whether it really is totally pointless.

👁 **Read Ecclesiastes 1 v 12–18**

ENGAGE YOUR BRAIN

▶ Where does the Teacher start his search? (v13)

▶ What are his conclusions? Jot them down below:

▶ Does human wisdom offer any answers?

PRAY ABOUT IT

Do you think that you know or can find out all the answers as long as you study hard enough, read enough books, get the best degree, listen to the most impressive philosophers? Ask God to give you the humility to listen to and accept His wisdom.

▶ Who is behind all of this frustration? (v13)

▶ Why might that be?

Look back to the beginning of the Bible and you'll see just why life is so frustrating. By rejecting the Maker's instructions (Genesis 3), human beings were doomed to frustration and conflict.

▶ If the frustration and pointlessness of our human experience is from God, does that give us any hope?

The Bible storyline is all about how God solves the problem of Genesis 3 (human sin). So bear with Ecclesiastes as the Teacher looks for answers. Only God has them.

THE BOTTOM LINE

Human wisdom is not the answer.

→ TAKE IT FURTHER

Human wisdom v God's wisdom on page 123.

79

Pleasure trip

The quest for meaning: episode two.
OK, so human wisdom failed to provide any answers, but how about living life to the max? Will that give life meaning?

Read Ecclesiastes 2 v 1–11

ENGAGE YOUR BRAIN

▶ What was the Teacher's aim? (v3)

▶ How did he go about it (v2)?
▶ What activities did he try? List them below and then try to write down a modern equivalent:

▶ v3

▶ v4

▶ v7

▶ v8

▶ What were his conclusions? (v11)

Look at all the things you wrote above. If you tried to find ultimate meaning in any or all of these things, they would prove just as empty and meaningless.

TALK IT OVER

Is it wrong to enjoy life? Are money and possessions bad? Talk it over with another Christian. 1 Timothy 6 v 6–10 and v17–19 might help.

PRAY ABOUT IT

Jesus once said: *'What good is it for a man to gain the whole world, yet forfeit his soul?'* (Mark 8 v 36). The answer to life's questions can't be found in drink, drugs, designer clothes or driving fast cars. Ask Jesus to help you keep your eyes fixed on what really matters.

THE BOTTOM LINE

The point of life isn't just to have a good time. Live life today for what really matters.

➔ TAKE IT FURTHER

Going to page 123 won't be meaningless, I promise.

80 | What's the point?

Who would you rather be? A respected, God-fearing professor at the world's best university? Or a homeless drug addict who curses God? Keep pondering that as we read on...

👁 Read Ecclesiastes 2 v 12–23

ENGAGE YOUR BRAIN

🔹 Who is better off? The wise man or the fool? (v13)

🔹 Are you sure? (v14)

🔹 What's the big problem for both? (v16)

🔹 How does this make the Teacher feel? (v 17–23)

It hardly seems fair, does it? However sensible you are, whatever you achieve, you'll end up the same way as the most hopeless loser. Death is the great leveller — everyone must face it in the end. No wonder the Teacher is so depressed. Look at the words he uses: *'hates life'*, *'despair'*, *'pain'*, *'grief'* and, of course, *'meaningless'*.

PRAY ABOUT IT

If you ever feel like this, then don't despair because:

a) you're absolutely right! Death was not part of God's original creation — it sucks.

b) one day death will be destroyed — Jesus has already conquered it! Talk to Him about how you feel about it all.

👁 Read verses 24–26

🔹 What does the Teacher decide is the right perspective to have on life? (v24)

🔹 What gifts does God give? (v26)

THE BOTTOM LINE

We will all die, but it's how we live that matters.

→ TAKE IT FURTHER

More pointers on page 123.

81

About time

Time for one of the greatest poems of all time. About time.

👁 Read Ecclesiastes 3 v 1–8

ENGAGE YOUR BRAIN

▶ What's your reaction to this poem?

▶ How much control do we have over the actions in v2–8?

▶ What does this teach us about human beings?

▶ Read verses 9–15

Notice that the Teacher asks the same question again in v9 — what's the point? See how he answers it this time.

▶ Who's in charge of life? (v11)

▶ What's the problem for human beings? (v11)

This perfectly sums up the frustration of human experience. We were made for an eternity with God, but we are limited by our short life-spans and the sin that takes over our lives. We can't see the big picture, but we know God is out there.

SHARE IT

The writer Oscar Wilde once said: *'We are all in the gutter but some of us are looking at the stars'*. Can you talk to a friend today about the sneaking suspicion we all have that there must be more to life than what we see here and now?

▶ How should we respond to life and to God? (v13-15)

PRAY ABOUT IT

Are you thankful for what God gives you every single day? Do you accept that He's in charge? Do you revere Him/honour Him? Pray about all those things now.

👁 Read verses 16–22

▶ What issue continues to worry the Teacher?

→ TAKE IT FURTHER

More on death and judgment on page 124.

82

Chasing after the wind

OK, so we've established the best way to live - thankful, honouring God - but how many people actually do it?

👁 **Read Ecclesiastes 4 v 1–3**

ENGAGE YOUR BRAIN

ⓓ Who seems worse off in this relationship? (v1)

ⓓ But what do they both have in common? (v1)

ⓓ What is the Teacher's conclusion?

👁 **Read verses 4–12**

ⓓ What different attitudes can you see towards work? (v4–6)

ⓓ Why is being a loner so meaningless? (v7–8)

ⓓ What is better? (v9–12)

ⓓ Why?

👁 **Read verses 13–16**

ⓓ Who does the ex-jailbird replace?

ⓓ How does his rule begin? (v15)

ⓓ How does it end? (v16)

ⓓ What is the Teacher's conclusion in v16 (no surprises here)?

Oppression, isolation, jealousy, laziness, greed, loneliness, short-lived political success. Can you see how all of these fail to live up to the standard set in chapter 3?

PRAY ABOUT IT

This is what our fallen world looks like. Spend some time praying about current situations (both close to home and in the news) that look like the situations in chapter 4.

GET ON WITH IT

Do verses 4–6 sound familiar? Do you want to do better than other people? Do you envy them their gifts and abilities? Take verse 6 to heart.

THE BOTTOM LINE

None of us live up to God's standard.

➡ TAKE IT FURTHER

Run to page 124.

83 Fools rush in

It's not just in normal everyday life that we fall short of God's standards. Take a look at what goes on even when people are claiming to worship God.

👁 Read Ecclesiastes 5 v 1–7

ENGAGE YOUR BRAIN

D *What advice does the Teacher give to people approaching God? (v1–2)*

D *Why is this so important?*

GET ON WITH IT

Look at verse 1 again. Are you really listening to God? Now? Make sure you keep listening to what He has to say as you read the Bible.

D *How does a fool behave? (v2–6)*

In the Bible, the word *'fool'* doesn't just mean someone who is a bit dumb. It is someone who offends God — they do wrong (v1) and sin (v6). God has no pleasure in them (v4); in fact he's angry with them (v6).

D *What's the right response before God? (v7)*

As Christians, we have the huge privilege of having God as our heavenly Father. But we need to remember He is also the Lord of the universe, and give Him the right amount of respect.

PRAY ABOUT IT

Does this challenge you? To see how these truths should shape your prayers take a look at Matthew 6 v 7–13.

THE BOTTOM LINE

Stand in awe of God.

➜ TAKE IT FURTHER

Check out page 124.

84 | Enjoy it while it lasts

You've probably noticed the same ideas cropping up again and again in Ecclesiastes. In some ways it seems a bit like a downwards spiral, but hang on in there, it's not hopeless...

👁 Read Ecclesiastes 5v8 – 6v2

ENGAGE YOUR BRAIN

▶ *Remember the right way to live? (Ecclesiastes 3 v 12–14)*

▶ *Can you find a similar idea in chapter 5?*

▶ *What fact does 5 v 18–19 remind us of?*

PRAY ABOUT IT

Stop for a minute and thank God for everything He has given you — both material stuff and spiritual stuff (see Ephesians 1 v 3–14 for the latter).

▶ *What does it look like when people don't live with this attitude? (v8–17 and 6 v 1–2) Jot down some examples below:*

▶ *Does anything in these verses challenge you about your goals in life?*

👁 Read Ecclesiastes 6 v 3–12

▶ *What issue does the Teacher bring up again in v3–6 and v12? Sum it up in your own words.*

Death. Yet again, any glimpse of hope is snuffed out by the ultimate statistic: one in one people die. We're still living in that fallen Genesis 3 world.

▶ *What answer would a Christian have for v12?*

SHARE IT

The fact that Jesus is alive offers a sure and certain hope that death is not the end for those who follow Him. Who can you explain that to?

THE BOTTOM LINE

Life is a gift of God.

➔ TAKE IT FURTHER

More work on page 124.

85  Good mourning

Hands up if you think the Teacher can be a bit of an Eeyore at times? Well, maybe he's got good reason. Isn't it better to be realistic than blindly optimistic, ignoring the facts?

👁 Read Ecclesiastes 7 v 1–10

ENGAGE YOUR BRAIN

▶ Look at verses 1-4. What makes people think about what is important in life?

▶ Why is thinking about death good for you?

▶ Do any of the sayings in v5-10 challenge you?

Can you remember what the definition of a fool is in the Bible? Well, the definition of wisdom goes like this: *'The fear of the Lord is the beginning of wisdom'* (Proverbs 9 v 10). Bear that in mind as you...

👁 Read verses 11–29

▶ Jot down what you discover about...
People (v14, 18, 20, 29)

God (v13, 14, 29)

We're living in a fallen, sin-filled world. Verse 29 in particular is a huge reminder of what went wrong back in Genesis 3.

GET ON WITH IT

Look at verses 21 and 22. It's never nice when people talk about you behind your back. But be honest — how many times have you done the same? Ask for God's help to keep your mouth shut on those occasions.

SHARE IT

Can you get someone to acknowledge the truth of v20 this week? Can you find anyone who never sins? Who never lies, loses their temper or treats others unkindly?

THE BOTTOM LINE

No one is perfect.

→ TAKE IT FURTHER

More explanation on page 124.

86 Fair's fair

The good die young and the wicked are successful. It just doesn't seem fair. What exactly is going on in this crazy, mixed-up world of ours?

👁 Read Ecclesiastes 8 v 1–17

ENGAGE YOUR BRAIN

▶ *What hope does v1 offer?*

▶ *What problems do we see with human rulers and society? (v2–14)*

▶ *Why do we react so strongly against v14?*

▶ *If v14 was the end of the story, would it matter what we do in this life?*

▶ *What would it tell us about God?*

We hate injustice — from the toddler who cries: *'It's not fair'* to the angry protesters outside the high court who think the sentence is too lenient for a murderer... we want **justice**.

▶ *What flicker of hope do verses 12 and 13 offer?*

PRAY ABOUT IT

Thank God that He is a God of justice. Thank Him that our actions do matter and that He will not let evil go unpunished forever.

TALK IT OVER

People often say that because bad things happen in this world then God either can't exist, or is powerless to stop things or He just doesn't care. Chat with another Christian about how you could answer these claims using the Bible.

▶ *Read v1 again, then look at v16–17. Is there any hope for us?*

▶ *If so, where can it be found? (Look back at v15 as well)*

THE BOTTOM LINE

Justice may be delayed but it is coming...

→ TAKE IT FURTHER

Feel life's unfair? Try page 124.

87 Out of control

Today, Jenna might win the lottery or she might get knocked down by a bus. But we're not living in a world of random chance. OK, so we don't always know what's going to happen next, but Someone does...

👁 Read Ecclesiastes 9 v 1–12

ENGAGE YOUR BRAIN

- ▶ What facts about human existence do verses 1–3 remind us of?

- ▶ What do we learn about God?

- ▶ What is the Teacher's answer to the inevitability of death? (v4–6)

- ▶ What is the Teacher's answer to the frustrations of life here and now? (v7–10)

- ▶ Who gives us everything?

- ▶ Can you find any similar verses as you look back over previous chapters?

- ▶ But what does the Teacher remind us of once again? (v11–12)

Remember the advice in chapter 7? Reminding ourselves that we'll die one day will help us live wisely now.

PRAY ABOUT IT

Thank God for what He has given you in life. Ask Him to help you enjoy it — not to be unsatisfied, always wanting more, or complaining about what you don't have.

TALK IT OVER

If you knew you were going to die tomorrow, (or you knew that Jesus would be coming back tomorrow), how different would the next 24 hours look in your life? Discuss your answer with a Christian friend.

THE BOTTOM LINE

We don't know the future, but God does.

→ TAKE IT FURTHER

Labour's lost love — page 124.

88

Be wise

Nobody wants to be a fool — but we often make fools of ourselves. Here are some of the Teacher's top tips for living wisely.

👁 **Read Eccles' 9 v 13 – 10 v 20**

ENGAGE YOUR BRAIN

▶ *Read through the whole section and see if you can find a verse or sentence which summarises the main point here. Write it below:*

Fill in the table below:

How does a fool behave?	Verses	How might you behave like this?

And then this one:

How does a wise person behave?	Verses	How might you learn from this?

You know what you need to do and what you need to avoid. Ask for God's help.

→ **TAKE IT FURTHER**

Follow the fool for loads more unfoolish advice on page 124.

89 | Just do it

With all this talk of life's meaninglessness it would be pretty easy to sit around feeling crippled by doubt and worry. Amazingly, that's not the way the Teacher says we should live...

Read Ecclesiastes 11 v 1–6

ENGAGE YOUR BRAIN

▶ What are we told to do in verses 1, 2 and 6?

▶ Why? (v2–5)

▶ Does not knowing what's around the corner make you over-cautious or do you make the most of every moment?

PRAY ABOUT IT

Take some time out to really think through the last question. Do you tend to worry about what the future holds? Will you actively trust God for exam results, job interviews, doctors' diagnoses, or whatever lies in store for you? Ask for His help to do that and make the most of life now!

▶ What does verse 5 remind us about God?

As Christians, we know that we can trust God entirely — He hasn't just created us but also redeemed us. He keeps His promises and works for our good in all things. And if we ever doubt that He cares for us, we just need to look back at the cross and see what Jesus did for us.

So how much more should we be trusting Him and living all out for Him today?

GET ON WITH IT

▶ How can you live all out for God, trusting Him and living as He wants, this week?

THE BOTTOM LINE

Don't be scared to live — God is in control.

➡ TAKE IT FURTHER

Face the future on page 125.

90 | Be joyful

As we reach the last few verses of Ecclesiastes, the Teacher reaches the conclusion of his argument — this life is fallen and frustrating, but God is in control. So be wise, be bold and now... be joyful.

👁 Read Ecclesiastes 11 v 7–10

ENGAGE YOUR BRAIN

▶ Does v7 sound like the Teacher's usual advice?!

▶ What is the downside to this advice? (v8b)

▶ What is the advice in v9?

▶ But what should inform the way we live and what we find joy in (v9b)?

▶ What really makes you happy? Sporting victories? Great music? Your boyfriend/girlfriend? People becoming Christians?

So even though you may be young and healthy, remember that one day you will die and face God's judgment. If you're wise, that will shape how you live now.

SHARE IT

Do your friends realise we will all face God one day? Judgment is not a popular truth. How can you explain it in a way people will understand?

PRAY ABOUT IT

We will all face judgment, but for some of us, Jesus has already taken the punishment we deserve. Pray for your friends who are not living for God now — ask Him to save them so that one day they can face Him unafraid because they are trusting in Jesus.

THE BOTTOM LINE

Live life now, in the light of eternity.

→ TAKE IT FURTHER

A little bit more on page 125.

91

Starting young

Wimbledon champions, chess grand masters, musical prodigies. What do they all have in common? Well, they started learning their skills when they were young.

👁 Read Ecclesiastes 12 v 1–8

ENGAGE YOUR BRAIN

▶ *What do you think it means to remember your Creator?*

▶ *Why is it important to start now while you're young?*

If you've grown up in a Christian home, or been a Christian since you were quite young, then maybe you think your testimony (story of how you became a Christian) is pretty boring. But be encouraged — you started to learn life's most important lesson early on!

SHARE IT

What would you say to someone who said: *'There'll be time to think about religion and God when I get old and near to dying; I'm not going to waste time on it now.'* How could what you've learned in Ecclesiastes help you?

PRAY ABOUT IT

Look at the images of growing old and decaying (v2-5). Pray now for people you know in your church and family who are facing the illnesses and worries of old age.

▶ *Look at verses 7 and 8 again. We've already seen that 'meaningless' = 'fallen', so what other echoes of Genesis 3 can you see?*

▶ *How will you remember God in everything?*

THE BOTTOM LINE

Put God first now, while you are young.

➔ TAKE IT FURTHER

Keep going... to page 125.

92 End of the road

Well done for sticking with Ecclesiastes! Read the Teacher's final words to find out whether everything really is meaningless after all.

👁 Read Ecclesiastes 12 v 9–14

ENGAGE YOUR BRAIN

▶ What do we learn about the Teacher? (v9–10)

▶ So why should we listen to him?

▶ Who gave him his wisdom (v11)?

▶ So how seriously should we take it?

Our Creator God (12 v 1) is also our Shepherd (see also Psalm 23, Ezekiel 34 v 11–16 and John 10 v 11–18).

▶ How does this truth encourage you?

▶ So what is the Teacher's big conclusion? (v13)

▶ What do you think it means to 'fear God'?

▶ What is the motivation to live like this? (v14)

It seems strange that the big answer to life's pointlessness is judgment. It certainly isn't the usual place to look for hope and meaning. But think about it — God cares about right and wrong, God won't let evil go unpunished, God will be completely fair.

SHARE IT

Do you know anyone who says they're an atheist? Now there's a world view that really is meaningless. No such thing as right or wrong, no justice, just a bunch of random events with no purpose. Think how you could challenge them to explain why they believe that.

PRAY ABOUT IT

Thank God for what He's been teaching you through Ecclesiastes.

→ TAKE IT FURTHER

The final word is on page 125.

TAKE IT FURTHER

If you want a little more at the end of each day's study, this is where you come. The TAKE IT FURTHER sections give you something extra. They look at some of the issues covered in the day's study, pose deeper questions, and point you to the big picture of the whole Bible.

EXODUS
Exit strategy

1 – EXTERMINATE!
Read verses 15–16, 22

▷ *What New Testament story does this remind you of?*

Read Matthew 2 v 13–18

When Jesus was born, Herod feared for the safety of his throne so he ordered all boys under two to be slaughtered. Disgusting. Throughout Exodus, Moses will remind us of God's perfect Rescuer — Jesus Christ.

2 – WATER BABY
Read Hebrews 13 v 5–6

▷ *What is the great news for God's people? (v5)*

▷ *What will it help them do? (v5)*

▷ *So what can Christians say with confidence? (v6)*

3 – ON THE RUN
Read Acts 7 v 17–29

▷ *What time was getting nearer?*

▷ *How is Moses described? (v20)*

▷ *How did God prepare Moses for his future work? (v22)*

▷ *What surprised Moses? (v25)*

Moses had a really weird upbringing. But despite 40 years living with Egyptians, he knew he was really a Hebrew — one of God's people. All the time, God was preparing him for the amazing work He had in store for Moses. Little did Moses know what God had planned for him.

4 – CRY FOR HELP
Read Matthew 6 v 5–8

How amazing is verse 8. Get it lodged in your heart. God knows what His people need before they ask Him. Take that in!

▷ *Will this change the way you pray about your problems?*

▷ *Why does it help to remember God's care in the past — throughout history and in your life so far?*

5 – WARNING: BUSH FIRE
Read verses 2–3 again

Fire was an Old Testament symbol of God's presence with His people. Sneak ahead to these verses in Exodus:

Exodus 13 v 21–22
Exodus 19 v 18
Exodus 32 v 10

It showed God's holiness and His anger in the face of sin. That's why Moses was told to keep well back.
Check out Hebrews 12 v 28–29

6 – I AM WHO I AM

Read verses 13–15 again
Hebrew names aren't just names — they explain something about the person. It's the same with God's name. *I AM* (v14) and *THE LORD* (v15) show He's the God who has kept His promises to Abraham, Isaac and Jacob. This great God is reliable and trustworthy!

Because of Jesus and His death in our place, we can be even more confident that God is completely reliable and keeps His promises.

7 – BACK TO THE FUTURE

Want to see how accurate God's predictions/promises were?
Read verses 16–18 then Exodus 4 v29–31
Read verses 18–19 then Exodus 5 v 1–2
Read verse 20 then flick through chapters 7–12
Read verses 21–22 and then Exodus 11 v 1–3

8 – EXCUSE ME

▶ How is it encouraging that God could still use disobedient servants like Moses in His work?
▶ What excuses do you make for not living God's way?
▶ What are your excuses for keeping quiet about Jesus?

Read Matthew 28 v 18–20
Most of us probably need to take both this command and this promise more seriously.

9 – THE WANDERER RETURNS

Read verse 21
How could God punish Pharaoh when God had hardened his heart? Well, Exodus will show us that God made Pharaoh what he chose to be. See the different ways it's expressed in **Exodus 4 v 21, 7 v 13, and 8 v 15.**

Read Romans 1 v 24–28
God punishes the godless by making them what they want to be.

10 – THE FINAL STRAW

▶ How do you cope when life seems to get harder and God doesn't seem to be helping?
Spend some extra time praying that tough times would help you trust God more.

11 – POWERFUL PROMISES

Read verses 6–9 again
▶ What is God prepared to do for His people?
▶ Why?
▶ Which of these verses encourages you in your relationship with God?

12 – FEELING LISTLESS?

God uses His people to spread His Word. This is a two-edged sword. On the plus side, people come to faith through hearing God's Word. On the other hand, sometimes believers are called to preach to people who won't repent. For example, Jeremiah and Isaiah in the Old Testament.

Read Isaiah 6 v 8–10
God sent Isaiah to people who wouldn't listen to God's message. Moses' work in Egypt had a similar double result. Unbelievers, such as Pharaoh, were hardened in their unbelief and judged accordingly. In contrast, God's people were freed from slavery and oppression.

God will use His Word as He sees fit. Sometimes that means we'll have the huge pleasure of seeing people turn to Him; or it might mean it feels as if we're headbutting a brick wall. Our job is to obey and spread His Word. God does the rest.

13 – FLOOD OF BLOOD

Why not read all of 7 v 14 – 10 v 29 in one go?
As you do, look out for repeated phrases, like *'Pharaoh hardened his heart'* or *'just as the Lord had said'*. And notice Pharaoh's bargaining (8 v 25, v28, 10 v 11, v24) and see how Moses dealt with it.

And ask yourself...
▶ *Did Pharaoh ever truly repent?*
▶ *So what is repentance?*

▶ *How had Moses changed since chapters 1–6?*
▶ *Why were these judgments happening?*
▶ *Where is it leading?*

15 – NO FLIES ON MOSES

Read verse 19
The *'finger of God'* is a weird phrase to describe God at work. But it shows up elsewhere in the Bible:

Exodus 31 v 18
Luke 11 v 17–20

**Read Exodus 8 v 22–23
and then 1 Peter 2 v 9**
Just like the Israelites, believers today are God's people and have been set apart, called from the darkness of the world by the ruler of the universe. Doesn't that make you want to *'declare God's praises'*?

16 – BOILING POINT

Read Romans 3 v 23
Pharaoh ignored God's warning signs and was being punished for it. Ultimately it would end in death. We've been warned too — if we choose our own sinful way we face eternal death. Only if we accept God's gift through the death and resurrection of His Son Jesus will we receive eternal life.

111

2 TIMOTHY
Letter from death row

17 – FAN THE FLAME

Read verses 4 and 7

Tim was timid. And he was young
(1 Timothy 4 v 12) and often ill (1 Tim 5 v
23). Yet God used him as a leader.

▶ *Are you a bit of a Timothy?*
Young or weak or shy?

Then grab this letter with both hands.
And take to heart that you don't need
to be older, super-healthy or an extrovert
to be used by God.

18 – NO SHAME

Read verse 8 again

Tim was told not to be ashamed of Jesus
or Paul or the gospel. In the same way,
we're tempted to keep quiet about Jesus;
to be embarrassed about the Christians
we mix with; to water down the Bible's
teaching because we know it will offend
people.

**Now read Romans 1 v 16
and Mark 8 v 38**

▶ *Why mustn't we be ashamed?*

Read 2 Timothy 1 v 8–9

Paul's letter talks loads about the gospel.
But what is it? In short, it's God rescuing
us from sin and from the punishment of
eternal death we deserve for our sin. But
over to you: have a bash at explaining it
more fully using these verses.

The gospel forces us to admit:
a) we're all worse than we thought
b) we can't rescue ourselves
c) we'd be nowhere without the cross
d) we need personally to trust Christ.

19 – RIGHT GUARD

**Read verses 16–18 again
and then Matthew 25 v 34–40
and James 1 v 27**

Onesiphorus took visiting very seriously.

▶ *Is it a Christian's responsibility to visit
or look after others?*
▶ *What can you do and who for?*

20 – PASS IT ON

Read verse 2

See the gospel relay?
From Jesus to Paul (Galatians 1 v 11–12),
from Paul to Tim (2 Tim 1 v 13–14),
from Tim to 'reliable men' (2 Tim 2 v 2a),
from them to others (2 Tim 2 v 2b)

▶ *In what way are you continuing
the relay?*

Notice the big command and promise of
verse 7. How great is that? You do the
thinking: God will give you understanding.

21 – TO DIE FOR

Read verse 8

Why did Paul need to say *'Remember
Jesus Christ'*?
a) So Tim would always hold on to the
gospel.
b) So Tim would remember that suffering
was Jesus' way, so we should expect it in

the Christian life. No pain, no gain.

22 – UNASHAMED WORKMAN

Read verse 18
and then Ephesians 2 v 6
and Colossians 3 v 1–4

In one sense, the resurrection *has* happened. Christ has been raised and His people have *'risen'* with Him. But our bodily resurrection is still to come.

🔹 *What are some wrong ideas about God that are around in the world and in the church?*

🔹 *How are you influenced by such wrong teachings?*

23 – RUN AWAY!

Read verses 15–21

What a privilege for Christians — being useful to Jesus. Notice the condition that Paul sets down? Being *'clean'* — sticking to the gospel, sticking to living a pure life.

🔹 *How can you be more 'clean'?*

Read verse 22

We're not alone in fleeing evil and chasing holiness. All Christians (those *'who call on the Lord'*) face this challenge too. We can encourage each other and help each other along. That's why it's great to meet and chat and pray regularly with other Christians.

24 – STUPID SQUABBLES

Read 2 Corinthians 10 v 1–5

The gospel is God's power: only the message of Jesus can change the pride

and unbelief in people's minds.

🔹 *What effect does gospel truth have? (v5)*

25 – TERRIBLE TIMES

Read Matthew 7 v 15–20

In the Old Testament, prophets spoke for God.

🔹 *What does Jesus say will mark out false prophets? (v15)*

🔹 *What are their real aims?*

🔹 *How long does it take to see if a tree is good or not? (v16)*

🔹 *What can we be certain of? (v17–18)*

🔹 *What happens to trees with bad fruit? (v19)*

🔹 *So... how can you tell if someone is a good Bible teacher or not?*

26 – GOD'S GREAT WORD

Read verse 11

To find out what happened to Paul in these places, **read Acts 13 v 13 – 14 v 23**

Read 2 Timothy 3 v 12
and then John 15 v 18–20

🔹 *What's the expectation for Christians?*

🔹 *Why does the world hate them?*

27 – FIGHTING TALK

Read verse 2

🔹 *Do you talk about Jesus even when it's inconvenient or you don't feel like it?*

Read verses 3–5

Some people will believe anything but the gospel.

🔹 *In what four ways was Tim to respond*

to that? (v5)

▶ Did it involve hiding in a corner, avoiding controversy?

▶ How should you respond when friends 'turn aside to myths'?

Paul mentions these guys in passing, but most of them get mentioned elsewhere in the New Testament.

Demas — read Philemon v24

Demas was described as a 'fellow-worker' with Paul before he left him in the lurch. **Read 1 John 2 v 15–19**

Titus — the book after 2 Timothy is a letter from Paul to Titus. **Read Titus 1 v 4–5 and Galatians 2 v 1–5.**

Luke — writer of the Gospel named after him and the book of Acts.

Mark (also called John and John Mark) had been a valued member of Paul's group until they fell out in Cyprus. John Mark continued working with Barnabus, strengthening churches of new Christians.

Read Acts 13 v 13 and Acts 15 v 36–41. So it's a surprise that Paul asked Mark to join him at the end of his life. Touching.

Tychicus had travelled with Paul on his last journey to Jerusalem, and carried letters to Colosse and Ephesus for Paul. **See Acts 20 v 4, Colossians 4 v 7 and Ephesians 6 v 21.**

Crescens and Carpus don't get mentioned elsewhere in the Bible.

Alexander may be the same one who was dissed in **1 Timothy 1 v 18–20**.

For more about the people mentioned at the end of 2 Timothy...

Priscilla and Aquila — Acts 18 v 18–26, Romans 16 v 3–5
Onesiphorus — 2 Timothy 1 v 16–18
Erastus — Romans 16 v 23, Acts 19 v 22
Trophimus — Acts 21 v 27–36

PSALMS

Some people read palms or tea leaves. Others look for signs in oddly shaped vegetables. But God says the main message from the created order is much clearer and on a grander scale.

Read Psalm 19 v 1–6 again

All this talk of voices in the sky can seem a bit far fetched. Can we really tell much about God just by looking up?

Read Romans 1 v 18–25

▶ What can be clearly seen in God's creation? (v20)

▶ What basic response is He looking for? (v21)

▶ What is it that holds people back? (v18)

Paul backs up David's idea that God is obvious. The simple beauty of what God has made should stir us to seek the Creator. The trouble is, the louder the noise of our evil behaviour, the more deaf we get to God's message.

Do your friends seem incapable of seeing what God has made crystal clear? Bring them in prayer to our eye-opening God.

31 – WINNING MENTALITY

A 3-year-old takes her pre-school artwork home. The random blobs and swirls would be unrecognisable if the picture wasn't clearly labelled with the word 'Dad'. Is this an accurate picture of the man? Hope not!

Read Hebrews 1 v 3

▶ What work has Jesus finished?
▶ What is He doing now?

Artists seem keen to show Jesus at His crucifixion. The importance of His suffering in our place should never be sidelined. But at His death He said, 'It's finished'. It's over. He's won. So how should we picture Jesus now?

Read Colossians 3 v 1–4

▶ Where should our hearts and minds be fixed?
▶ Where is Jesus?

Jesus came, not to big Himself up, but to lay Himself down. The Bible calls Him the suffering servant, the man of sorrows. But now He's alive and He's in charge. And when we see Him — forget the pain and anguish — He'll be stunning, awesome,

majestic. Don't wait for that final unveiling — worship Him now!

32 – THE SECRET OF SUCCESS

Once you've reached the snow-topped summit, the only way is down — unless you happened to bring a step ladder. How can you get higher than the highest?

Psalm 21 v 5–6 shows us the king's glory growing as a result of each triumph. An earthly commander-in-chief might carry golden treasures back home from every enemy palace conquered, but what does victory mean for King Jesus?

Read Philippians 2 v 5–11

▶ Already 100% God, what was Jesus' route to more greatness?
▶ How great is His name now?
▶ Where will He be worshipped?

Worshipping the saviour of the world won't always be a minority pastime. He's greater than all greatness, and one day everyone will see it.

33 – HEARTCRY OF A HERO

Immediately after impact, even a mild whack to the little toe can make you feel like giving up on life. Pain has a way of making anything good seem irrelevant.

Read Psalm 22 v 6–10

▶ What memories does he recall to help silence the critics and bullies?
▶ On a scale of 1 to 10 how easily is your faith derailed by grief and

115

disappointment?
(1 = your world crumbles at a broken nail)
(10 = you laugh off the deepest tragedy)

Hebrews 12 v 1-3
🔊 *What examples can inspire stamina in us?*
🔊 *What goal pushed Jesus through the pain barrier? (v2)*

So what's the worst thing you're suffering at the moment? Let Jesus' own words inspire you to ask God to help you keep going, living His way.

34 – OFF COURSE?
Paul's missions brought cities and nations their first taste of gospel glory. With such a history-making role, God made His route painless, right? Wrong!

Read 2 Corinthians 1 v 8–11
🔊 *What did Paul feel like giving up on?*
🔊 *Why might he be telling them this? For sympathy?*

The Christian life isn't supposed to be easy. Whether serving the homeless in hostile lands or serving hotdogs in town, when you live for Jesus, trouble happens.

🔊 *What was God's purpose in Paul's struggle?*
🔊 *Did Paul give up taking risks for Jesus? (v10)*

There's logic here. You can't know what resurrection is unless you, er, die first.

Well-timed trials will keep us humble and help us remember the source of power — the Lord. God's story line for David, for Paul and for us: we need Him. End of story.

'Apart from me you can do nothing'
(John 15 v 5).

35 – RED CARPET TREATMENT
God is moving in, and not just invisibly. The countdown to His return has already begun.

Read 2 Peter 3 v 11–14
🔊 *What kind of lives are prepared for God's coming?*
🔊 *What should our attitude be to the approaching events?*

🔊 *Be honest. What future events tend to define the course of your life?*
🔊 *How do thoughts of a dream job, a perfect partner or other ambition drive your actions?*

Now picture putting your efforts into a v14 style existence.
🔊 *How would life look different?*

JOHN
Famous last words

36 – THE TIME HAS COME

Look back at all the times Jesus has mentioned *'the time'* or *'the hour'*:

John 2 v 4
John 7 v 6
John 7 v 30
John 12 v 23, v27–28, v31–32,
and John 13 v 1.

37 – FAITHFUL FOLLOWERS

Take a deeper look at how God takes the initiative in saving us...

Romans 5 v 6–8
Ephesians 1 v 3–14 and 2 v 1–10.

38 – FACING FOES

In the New Testament *'the world'* means people living without God as their King.

▶ *How do you show that you are 'not of the world'?*

▶ *And have you seen examples of how the world hates those who are like Jesus and not like the world?*

Read verse 12 again
The one *'doomed to destruction'* refers to Judas Iscariot. Check out **Psalm 41 v 9 and John 13 v 18.**

39 – FAITH IN THE FUTURE

Is unity realistic when the worldwide church seems to have so much division and disagreement? Well, Jesus' prayer for unity will be answered ultimately in God's new heaven and earth, where all His people will be united in worshipping the Lord. For now, we've got to work at showing unity with other Christians, especially those who have different views on things that aren't central to Christianity.

Read Philippians 2 v 1–11
Pray that you and the Christians you know would show this kind of unity.

40 – FINAL FRONTIER

Check out 1 Corinthians 13, especially v8–13, and then talk openly with God.

41 – TIME FOR A REST

'The cup' is an Old Testament picture of God's anger and punishment.
Check out Isaiah 51 v 17 and 22,
Jeremiah 25 v 15,
Revelation 14 v 10 and 16 v 19.

42 – OUT IN THE COLD

Ever behaved/felt like Peter did? Why be ashamed of Jesus? Ask God to forgive you. And wait for the relief that's coming in chapter 21...

Why not try reading some Christian biographies about people who stood firm for Jesus even if it meant dying? Try *'Travel With the Martyrs of Mary Tudor'* by Andrew Atherstone. And check out the incredible true story on page 36.

43 – TRIAL AND ERROR

Look back through John's Gospel — what was it about Jesus' teaching that made the Jewish leaders so angry?

Read verse 19

Think why Annas quizzed Jesus on these two topics. Maybe he wanted to find out the size of Jesus' following (in case of any rebellion) and exactly what Jesus was claiming.

In trials like this, witnesses were usually questioned, not the defendant. But this trial was completely illegal and one-sided.

🔘 What's great about the way Jesus handles this assault? (v23)

🔘 What can you learn form Jesus about the way to handle angry opposition?

45 – PLOTS AND PLANS

Why did Jesus need to be crucified rather than executed another way?

Read Deuteronomy 21 v 22–23
and see if you can work it out.
Galatians 3 v 13 might help.

46 – THE TRUTH IS OUT THERE

Read Romans 1 v 18–32

🔘 Why is God angry with people? (v18–19)

🔘 Why should we know better than walking out on God? (v20)

🔘 Instead, how do people treat God? (v21–23)

🔘 How does God respond? (v24)

See the same pattern in v25–27 and again in v28–32. *'God gave them over...'* (v24, v26, v 28) — God punishes those who reject Him, by letting them have what they want. They choose to be ruled by sin and have nothing to do with God. So they're punished by being ruled by sin and separated from God forever. Sad but true.

47 – TERRIBLE TORTURE

Look at the description of Jesus in **Revelation 1 v 12-18** and realise how awful v2-3 are.

48 – DEATH SENTENCE

Look again at the whole story of Jesus' arrest, trial and execution — how many times can you spot a reference to it being part of God's plan, prophesied in the Scriptures?

EXODUS

49 – HAIL TO THE KING

Read verse 13

'Let my people go, so that they may worship me.' Freed so they can serve God? Isn't that a contradiction of terms? Not according to these Bible bits...

Read Galatians 5 v 13, Hebrews 9 v 14 and 1 Peter 2 v 16–17

🔘 How does serving God bring freedom?

🔘 Can you think of times when serving God has given you freedom?

50 – DAY OF THE LOCUST

Read verses 1–2 again
God gives two reasons for the plagues being brought against Egypt. Firstly, it was their punishment for rejecting God and mistreating His people.

Secondly, the plagues were for the benefit of the Israelites. They teach God's people about His character — that He deals harshly with sin, performs amazing miracles, and is the one and only God, in control of everything. Check out what Jethro said when he heard about the plagues and God rescuing His people…

Read Exodus 18 v 9–12
▶ How did he react?
▶ What did he learn about God?

52 – FINAL WARNING

Read verses 2–3
and then Genesis 15 v 13–14
Centuries before Moses, God had told Abram this would happen. God had promised to punish the nation who enslaved His people and He promised that His people would come out Egypt with great possessions. God always keeps His promises.

53 – MAKING A MEAL OF IT

Jesus was known as the **Lamb of God**. Check out these amazing Bible verses about Him:

Isaiah 53 v 7
John 1 v 29
1 Corinthians 5 v 7
1 Peter 1 v 17–21

54 – FEAST FIRST

Read 1 Corinthians 5 v 7–8
▶ Since Jesus died in their place, how should Christians behave?

Most Christians don't celebrate Passover or avoid yeast any more. Jesus gave them a new meal to eat and to remember His death in their place.

Read Luke 22 v 7–19

55 – TIME TO GO

Read verse 42
It was the dead of night, but God doesn't sleep or slumber — He protects His people 24/7.

Read Psalm 121
▶ How is God described? (v2)
▶ How detailed is God's care?
▶ How protective?
▶ How personal?

56 – GOD'S PEOPLE

God first commanded His people to get circumcised back in Genesis 17.

Read Genesis 17 v 9–14
▶ Why did God want His people circumcised? (v11)

It was a sign of God's covenant. Like wearing a badge which said 'Hey! I'm living under God's care with God's people!' Nice one. But it wasn't a ticket to heaven: circumcised or not, you still had to trust and obey God (as Abram did).

57 – REMEMBER REMEMBER
Read verses 8 and 14
God's people were always to remember the Exodus rescue. And to explain its meaning to their kids.

- Are you able to explain why Jesus' death is so important?
- What does Jesus' death and resurrection mean for you?

58 – GOD'S GUIDANCE
Read Hebrews 11 v 22

- How did Joseph's request show His faith in God?
- How much are you trusting God at the moment?
- How much are you relying on yourself or other people?
- What things do you need to hand over to God and trust Him about?

Talk about your answers to these questions with God right now.

59 – IN A TIGHT SPOT
Read verse 4
God's purpose and plan is that He should be praised. That's not selfish. He's all-powerful God. He does so much for His undeserving people. So we *should* praise Him.

60 – WALKING THROUGH WATER
Read Hebrews 10 v 31
The Egyptians discovered this to be terrifyingly true. One day, everyone who has lived their lives without God will discover it too.

- What does this make you want to say to your non-Christian friends and family?

61 – SING WHEN YOU'RE WINNING
For another burst of praise to God, **read Ephesians 1 v 3–14**

- Why is God worth shouting about? (v3)
- Jot down all that God has done for us (v4–14):

- Given all that, how should we respond?

62 – RAISE THE PRAISE

Read verse 18
and then Psalm 9 v 1–11

▶ What did God do to His people's enemies? (v3–6)

▶ What great truths do we learn about God here? (v7–10)

▶ What should our response be? (v11)

Use verses 7–10 to praise God right now.

63 – THREE DAYS LATER…

Read verse 26
and then Psalm 119 v 33–80

Read the verses slowly. Think which verses you can say honestly to God, and read them aloud to Him.

JOHN

64 – NOTICE THE NOTICE

The other Gospel accounts give more detail about the two men crucified either side of Jesus.

Read Matthew 27 v 38–44
and Luke 23 v 39–43

▶ What do these two men teach us about
a) ourselves?
b) Jesus?

65 – ALL PART OF THE PLAN

Take a look at two more predictions of Jesus' death in **Isaiah chapter 53** and **Psalm 22 v 18**.

66 – FINISHED

Lots of Christian songs and hymns include Jesus' final cry of *'It is finished'*.

▶ Can you think of any?

▶ Why do you think this is an encouraging thing for Christians to sing about?

67 – DEAD CERTAIN

Time to check out more incredible things predicted about Jesus, hundreds of years earlier: **Psalm 34 v 19–20**
          Zechariah 12 v 10
          Isaiah 53 v 1–6

Get hold of a book that goes through all the evidence for Jesus' death and resurrection for yourself and/or a friend. Josh McDowell's *Evidence for the Resurrection* is a good place to start.

68 – DEAD AND BURIED?

It's easy to get over familiar with the accounts of Jesus' death.

▶ How will you avoid this?

▶ How can you be amazed by it once more and not take it for granted?

Make a list of all the objections people might have to the resurrection. See if you can answer them from John 19–21.

69 – RISE AND SHINE

For more on what Jesus' resurrection accomplished check out **1 Corinthians 15 v 12–25**.

▶ *So, says Paul, if there was no resurrection from the dead at all, what would be the logical conclusion*
• about Jesus? (v13, v 16)
• about Paul's whole life? (v14)
• about Christians' faith in Jesus? (v14)
• about God? (v15)
• about Christians' relationship with God? (v17)
• about Christians already dead? (v18)

▶ *What facts was Paul convinced of? (v20–22)*

▶ *How would you sum up why it's vitally important that Jesus DID rise from death?*

70 – HE'S ALIVE!

Spend some time thinking about what it means for you that Jesus is alive. Talk to God about it.

71 –FORGIVEN FOLLOWERS

The risen Jesus transformed lives — compare the disciples of verse 19 with **Acts 4 v 1–21**. It's amazing stuff.

72 – TRUST THOMAS

Why not chat to someone you know who isn't a Christian? Ask them what evidence they would need to believe Jesus rose from the dead. Show them how much evidence God has already given them.

Scribble down some of the things you'd say. For extra pointers, check out the **Tricky** article on page 90.

73 – REASON FOR WRITING

Skim through John's Gospel and see how many references you can find to *'life'*.

John wants his readers to trust Jesus — He's the Christ, the long-awaited ruler and rescuer who'd reveal God to the world and bring *life*: the privilege of knowing God, being right with Him, both now and eternally.

▶ *What has John's Gospel done for you?*
▶ *Will you thank God?*

74 – WHAT A CATCH!

Read 1 Peter 5 v 7.
▶ *Do you believe that?*
▶ *Do you do that?*

Spend some time now casting all your anxieties and worries on Him in prayer.

75 – PETER PARDONED

Peter served Jesus for over 30 years as a shepherd of Jesus' sheep — he even wrote some letters about it.

Have a read of **1 Peter and 2 Peter**. It's inspiring, challenging stuff. Have a pen and paper to hand to jot down what God teaches you as you read Peter's letters.

Read verse 18

Incredibly, Peter lived and served Jesus for over 30 years with this prediction hanging over him. See what he had to say about suffering: **1 Peter 4 v 12–16**.

Look back over John's Gospel.

D *What have you learnt?*
D *What has challenged you?*

Thank God for it.

ECCLESIASTES
Everything's
meaningless

Verse 1 shows the sort of book Ecclesiastes is — a 'wisdom' book. And just so you can impress your mates, *'Ecclesiastes'* is the Greek equivalent of the Hebrew word for *'Teacher'*. Clever.

The book's best understood as describing life in a fallen world (a world that's rejected God and so come under His judgment), rather than being about life without God. Ecclesiastes shows the battle of trying to trust God and understand His ways when life seems hard, frustrating and unfair. So in v1–11, the Teacher is saying *'Life seems pointless even with God in it'*. But the New Testament tells us something very different. Keep coming to *Take it Further* for the New Testament view.

For more on God's wisdom versus human wisdom, **read 1 Corinthians 1v18 – 2v5**.

D *Why is God's wisdom so alien to us?*
D *Why is it better?*
D *What's God's method of saving people? v28–31*
D *What can no Christian ever claim? (v30–31)*

D *Have you ever read any of those lists of the top ten things to do before you die?*
D *What do you think of the idea behind the lists?*
D *What would be on your list now you've heard the Teacher's conclusion?*

Death was not part of God's original creation and will not be part of the new creation either.

Read Revelation 20 v 11 – 21 v 4

Spend some time praying for anyone you know who has lost someone recently.

Read Ecclesiastes 2 v 24

'The basics of life are sweet and good... what spoils them is our hunger to get more out of them than they can give.'
Do you agree with that?

So eat, drink and be merry. Not because tomorrow you die, but because God's given us those things to enjoy — so do so! In a way that pleases Him, obviously!

81 – ABOUT TIME

Death is still a problem.

▶ But what glimmer of hope does the Teacher offer us in v17?

▶ How would you answer the questions in verses 21 and 22?

82 – CHASING AFTER THE WIND

For a New Testament look at a world rejecting God, **check out Romans 1 v 18–32**.

▶ Look at your school, college, workplace, country... how does it reflect these verses?

83 – FOOLS RUSH IN

▶ Do you need to repent of the way you behave towards God?

▶ Do you take Him for granted? Treat Him without much respect?

Read Revelation 1 v 9–18 and think about who Jesus really is.

▶ How will you change the way you behave towards God?

84 – ENJOY IT WHILE IT LASTS

Ask God to make you the sort of person mentioned in 5 v19.

▶ Will you be happy with what you have, not wanting more or envying others?

▶ Will you be happy in your work and studies, no matter how difficult it is or how annoying other people are?

85 – GOOD MOURNING

Verses 11–22 can be summed up by one question:

▶ Which would you prefer: £1000 or some good advice?

If you took the money, go back to the beginning of Ecclesiastes and start again!

Look at verse 20 again
Then read Romans 3 v 9–26

▶ Have you really accepted this?

▶ Why is Jesus so special?

86 – FAIR'S FAIR

Again we're told that work (of any kind) may bring satisfaction, but will always be a sweat (see also Genesis 3 v 17–19).

87 – OUT OF CONTROL

Even though we can enjoy our work, it is often a real effort – compare 9 v 9 with Genesis 3 v 17–19.

▶ How will this realistic view help you in your work?

88 – BE WISE

The great thing about mistakes is to learn from the ones others make too — so you don't make so many yourself. Most of us probably laugh at fools (v3, v12–15), sneer at slobs (v18) and take pride in our own foresight (v8–11).

▶ But how are we more like these people than we admit?

▶ Why do you think the teacher is giving us all these proverbs?

It's probably got something to do with

wanting to show us how to live, and what to avoid in a frustrating, fallen world. And how to cope while we battle for answers to life's bigger questions.

▶ *Which of today's proverbs will change the way you behave?*

For more on wisdom and foolishness read **Proverbs chapter 1**.

89 – JUST DO IT
Read Romans 8 v 28–30
It reminds us that Christians are in safe hands now with a secure future ahead of us.

▶ *Do you really believe that?*
▶ *Could you learn these verses by heart?*

90 – BE JOYFUL

▶ *How is* **Philippians 4 v 4–5** *a Christian version of Ecclesiastes 11 v 9?*
▶ *How can you be a 'partner in the gospel' with other Christians?*
▶ *What will you do to make that happen?*

91 – STARTING YOUNG

Do you think it will be easier to live as a Christian once you leave home or go to university? Ask God to start shaping you into the person He wants you to be now.

92 – END OF THE ROAD

The Teacher began: *'Everything is meaningless'* in 1 v 2.

▶ *Has he provided answers to that?*
▶ *If so, what?*

Check out Psalm 49
It's got a similar flavour to Ecclesiastes.

Well done for making it through this hard-going book!

▶ *Will you thank God for the truths it's taught you?*
▶ *Will you ask God to help you be different as a result?*

125

RSVP

engage wants to hear from YOU!

▶ Share experiences of God at work in your life
▶ Any questions you have about the Bible or the Christian life?
▶ How can we make *engage* even better?

Email us — **engage@thegoodbook.com**

Or use the space below to write us a quick note. You can post it to:

engage 37 Elm Road, New Malden, Surrey, KT3 3HB, UK

In the next **engage**...

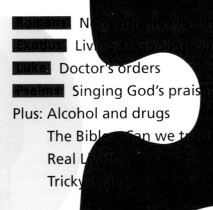

Romans News for the world

Exodus Living as God's people

Luke Doctor's orders

Psalms Singing God's praises

Plus: Alcohol and drugs

The Bible: Can we trust it?

Real Lives

Tricky...

Order **engage** now!

Make sure you order the next issue of engage. Or even better, grab a one-year subscription to make sure engage plops through your letterbox as soon as it's out.

Call us to order in the UK on **0845 225 0880**

International: **+44 (0) 20 8942 0880**

or visit your friendly neighbourhood website:

UK: www.thegoodbook.co.uk

USA: www.thegoodbook.com

Australia: **www.thegoodbook.com.au**